MW00654249

Lilacs to Share

& Shirts in the Refrigerator

Enjoy!

Rose Trochlil

by

Carol Deml Sisterman and Rose Deml Trochlil

Carol Sisterman

190

Copyright © 2013 by Carol Deml Sisterman and Rose Deml Trochlil

First Edition

All Rights Reserved

ISBN: 978-1-938911-51-4

Library of Congress Card Catalog Number: Pending

    I. Farm life: Mid-West United States--1940s and 50s
    II. Czechoslovakian recipes
    III. Minnesota history
    IV. Memoir
    V. Alcoholism
    VI. Bi-polar disorder
    VII. Changes in farming, education, family life, and the role of women

Initial Readers: Gail Kittleson and Ramona Morse
Writing Consultant: Susan Versley
Editor: Margaret Smolik
Final Reader: Kathleen Stauffer
Farm Sketch: Rose Deml Trochlil
Cover Design and Digital Imaging: Ken Small, Blue Springs, Missouri
Printers: Total Printing Systems

P.S. For those who would like to know more about Carol's life, e-mail her at: cas@myomnitel.com to request *Song of Joy: A Memoir* by Carol Sisterman. Also, a copy of Dad's book, *I Carried You*, can be requested through Carol's e-mail address.

ACKNOWLEDGEMENTS

We thank our husbands and families for their continuous support
and encouragement.

We thank Susan Versley, our editor for setting the direction of
our book.

Thank you to Gail Kittleson, Ramona Morse, Margaret Smolik,
and Kathleen Stauffer for reading and editing the work.

Thank you to Ken Small for creating the format and typesetting
of this book.

We thank you and appreciate the encouragement extended by
Alpha Writers, Internet friends and readers of Carol's earlier,
book, *Song of Joy*.

Most importantly, we thank God—Father, Son and Holy Spirit—
for the countless gifts we receive daily.

Barn, Garage, Milk House, Ramshackle Pig House, Granary, House, Biffy, Chicken House, Corncrib

INTRODUCTION

This book, *Lilacs to Share*, written by two Deml sisters began with a conversation about the buildings on their farm as they existed when the girls were young. The authors, Rose Deml Trochlil and Carol Deml Sisterman, lived on a farm near Owatonna in southern Minnesota in the 1940s and 50s. Neither has lived there since 1959. The farm was sold in 1969.

Whenever Rose returned to Minnesota for a visit with relatives, she drove by the farm to see the changes. Rose completed a watercolor painting—an overview of the farm as she recalled it from her childhood—and showed it to Carol. This sparked an idea for Carol who moderated a writing group at the time and was searching for a writing theme for the class. Ah ha. The inspiration came from the buildings! What memories do we have connected with each building? First we wrote separately about what we recalled—building by building. As we shared these chapters, more and more memories came to mind.

The story was written especially for Lori, our youngest sister, who was born when Rose was 20 and Carol 17. Lori did not share these early years. In addition, we decided to write for family, grandchildren, and for readers young and old, whether or not they lived on a small farm in the upper Midwest, to share and explain life on the farm before electricity, before indoor plumbing, before electric heat, before television and the electronic age. Photos and conversations make the account a unique portrayal of the era.

This story tells of a time when life was simpler and much harder physically, a time we recall fondly and hope you enjoy, also.

Lori

Carol Deml Sisterman   *Rose Deml Trochlil*

TABLE OF CONTENTS

Contents

HOPES AND DREAMS

In the mid-1800s, Czech immigrants began settling the areas called Litomysl and Saco/Moravia in Somerset Township, Steele County, Minnesota.

Our ancestors, Josef and Terezia Deml, great grandparents to our Dad, came from Czechoslovakia in 1884 and purchased their farmstead July 2, 1884, from Frank and Rosa Vesely. (Coincidentally, Dad, Lawrence Deml, was born July 2, 1913).

The Vesely-Deml family connections trace back to the 1800s in Bohemia, Czechoslovakia. Some of the Vesely brothers changed the spelling from Vesely to Wesely. Consequently, Mom's maiden name was Wesely. Once again a Wesely-Deml family tree established.

> **ROSE:** *When I was growing up, there was a popular song called "I'm My Own Grandpa." In the song we heard the words, "I'm my own grandpa. I'm my own grandpa. It really is funny but it really is true. I'm my own grandpa." This strikes my funny bone because, technically speaking, Dad is a third cousin once removed to Carol and me.*

As a child, Dad—Lawrence Deml—attended Holy Trinity Church in Litomysl, about five miles away from his home. Mom—Elsie Wesely—grew up in Saco (both

1

communities in Somerset Township about seven miles apart). St. Wenceslaus Church stood about a mile from Mom's childhood home, seven miles southwest of Owatonna, in the center of one of the first Czech settlements in Steele County.

During the years when Mom and Dad were growing up, Father John Nepomucene Pivo was pastor of Sacred Heart Church in Owatonna. Born in 1865 in Southern Bohemia, he later became pastor of Sacred Heart Church in 1891 and served not only the Czech population of Steele County (both St. Wenceslaus in Saco and Holy Trinity in Litomysl included), but also the flocks in Austin, Albert Lea, Waseca and New Richland. (And, most of his ministry, covering about 150 miles of territory, may have been accomplished on horseback.) He served the area from 1891 through September of 1936—about six months after Mom and Dad's wedding.

Father Pivo sometimes assigned baptismal names if he did not like the names chosen by the parents of the child to be baptized. When Mom was to be baptized, Father Pivo insisted that she must be called Elizabeth. Grandpa and Grandma Wesely were told they could call her Elsie—which was their choice, but her baptismal name would be that of a saint—not Elsie.

In those days, if farm children were needed, they stayed home to help the family. Contrast that with today's state requirement that children attend school until a given age.

In the 1920s Dad attended River Point, District 37, a two-room country school on the western edge of the Litomysl settlement. This country school had indoor plumbing, one of the few country schools with such accommodations. He spent his freshman and sophomore years at Owatonna High School.

Dad hoped to become an agriculture extension agent but had to leave school after his sophomore year of high school. Dad was the third oldest in a family of seven and the second-oldest boy. His older brother, Edward, married and moved onto his own farm, which meant the loss of a farm-hand. So, after finishing tenth grade, Dad had to stay home to help his father on the home place.

2

Deml's 20th Anniversary family photo: Back: Edward, Dad, Marie Front: Leonard, Grandpa Joseph, Babe, Joseph, Grandma Albina, Margaret

Mom attended a one-room country school, District 69 in Saco, for seven years. The area was known as Saco then, but was originally called Moravia after Frank Moravia, its first settler, who lived there in 1860. As a young girl, Mom dreamed of being a teacher. After Mom completed seventh grade, she looked forward to the coming school year. However, that summer twin sisters were born and, as the third oldest child and oldest girl at home, Mom was needed to help care for the little ones. There were now five boys and five girls in the family.

Mom's older sister, Leona had two consecutive sets of twins and Mom was again needed to help with the little ones. In exchange for babysitting and house work, Mom lived in town with Leona and was able to work in Owatonna—first at a café and later at the *Owatonna's Daily People's Press*. Dad was still working on the farm with his father.

Mom and Dad, now in their early twenties, met at a dance at the Auditorium Hall in Owatonna. They managed to spend time together. Eventually, their dancing and dating led to plans to marry.

CAROL: *When Mom and Dad approached Father Pivo and expressed their desire to be married, he*

3

said they could not, that they were too closely related. Church law required third cousin separation. Our parents' heritage fell within those guidelines.

Our parents, Lawrence and Elsie Deml, married on February 4, 1936, smack in the middle of the Great Depression, in Owatonna, Minnesota, the day of a severe blizzard.

No exotic island destination trip for this couple in February 1936. Dad had six brothers and sisters and Mom had nine brothers and sisters. Of these only about a dozen were able to attend the wedding at Sacred Heart Catholic Church.

> **CAROL:** *Originally, Mom and Dad's reception was to be held at the Wesely farm and a snowstorm prevented this. So, Grandma Wesely's lemon pies were left on the farm. Afterwards, Mom's youngest brother, Uncle Henry, ate so many pieces of lemon pie that in his later years he had a hard time looking at a lemon pie.*

Because of the blizzard, their reception took place at Aunt Leona's home rather than on the Wesely farm and only an uncle of Mom's attended the wedding dance.

> **ROSE:** *Mom told me that following the wedding ceremony she and Dad were seated for the wedding dinner. Dad lit a cigarette and the flame touched the edge of Mom's wedding veil and singed it.*
>
> *Almost a half century later, I was completing the final pressing of my daughter's wedding veil, and the phone rang. Oops, the iron scorched the veil while I talked on the phone. Expecting total dismay from my daughter, she surprised me by saying, "Oh, now my veil is just like Grandma's. Her veil, my veil—each scorched or torched on the wedding day."*

4

At last a new day and the folks began their wedding trip in a new pick-up truck that Dad purchased with his father's help. Dad's new truck had room for three, so three people went on a three-day honeymoon to the Twin Cities.

But it was not Dad's father but Mom's father who went on the honeymoon trip. In addition to savings Mom had from her work in Owatonna, she received a monetary wedding gift from her parents. On this trip, Mom selected a bedroom set, a gift from her parents, and dining room set with her savings.

> **CAROL:** *Grandpa Wesely subsidized their shopping spree, so he accompanied the couple on their trip to Minneapolis. What bridegroom today would tolerate having his father-in-law accompany the couple on their honeymoon?*

After their three-day honeymoon/shopping spree, the three began their return trip to Owatonna. They were stuck three vehicles behind a snow plow which spewed snow high above the snow banks. The snow reached the height of poled telephone wires, a snowfall record for many years before and after 1936.

Even without heavy snow, the trip from Minneapolis to Owatonna was a three-hour drive, unlike today's one-hour trip on the freeway. So, if someone (Dad) needed a potty break, he stopped his car, got out and went right there on the vast plain—in front of God and everyone following. Dad enjoyed telling this story. He claimed there were many cars behind their truck.

Mom and Dad settled on a typical 80-acre farm in southern Minnesota where land was neatly divided in square-mile sections of 640 acres each. This fertile area was very flat—more like Iowa corn country than The Land of the 10,000 Lakes that many folks imagine Minnesota to be. The house sat on a slight rise facing east, bordered by a busy north-south highway, then simply called Highway 65 (instead of US Highway 65), now known as County Road

5

45. It was a rectangular farm extending one-half mile to the west. A grove of trees surrounding the farm sheltered the buildings from western winter winds.

Farm families of that era were self-sustaining. Woods were cleared to provide more tillable land. Crops were grown as cattle feed and later as cash crops. People grew or raised the vast majority of what they needed to live. Most had a few cows, a team of horses, a few pigs, and a dozen chickens. Cattle provided milk and meat. More cattle meant more milk to sell and, possibly, more animals to sell. Both were sources of cash.

Within eight years of their marriage, Rose, Carol and Cathy were born. The Deml's family grew and changed just as the buildings and all farm life would change in the coming years.

THE BARN

When people think of farming, the barn is the image that usually springs to mind first with good reason. The barn is huge, multi-purpose, fascinating—and absolutely vital to the farm's operation. Not only is it the main location for housing animals and their food and bedding, it is an area in which a lot of important work happens. In addition, it's a great place for children to play—and a place where the Deml sisters had a few close calls. Danger is ever-present on a farm.

Our barn was not the storybook red-and-white one many people picture but the more typical long, two-level structure of weathered gray wood with no trim around the windows. Still, to the girls it was a castle of fascination, growth, amusement, hard work and wonder—Carol's favorite farm building. It sat on a high rise above the other buildings. Inside, the animals were safe and warm. It did what most barns do: stored feed, hay and straw, and housed and protected the big animals as well as a collection of smaller ones (some welcome, some not).

The barn was also smelly—but in a good way. All sorts of smells emanated from it each evoking its own special memory: silage (heavy-duty work), fresh hay (mmm), oiled leather harness (rides in the wagon or on horseback). And, of course, there was also the ever-present odor of great amounts of manure from cows, horses, and pigs (memories of caring for the animals, and of a lot of work mucking out

stalls). Some of that manure smelled just right for a barn—
it was even sort of reassuring. To add to the mix was the
occasional whiff of leavings of bats, birds, cats, kittens and
dogs (you never forgot you were on the farm).

On the second floor of the barn, a huge door yawned
wide (like a hippopotamus' mouth, it seemed to Carol).
Whenever that huge maw was open, it meant a lot of work
for that was where hundreds of bales of hay and straw were
fed into the hayloft—all of them needed to feed and bed the
animals.

> **CAROL:** *One sunny summer day, when Cathy and I
> were seven and ten, we sat on the ledge of the mammoth
> door, dangling our legs. We were smoking and talking
> (probably planning our weddings or deciding how many
> children we would like to have). We paid no attention
> to the lengthening ashes on our cigarettes. Suddenly,
> I realized that we'd dropped ashes between the slats
> of wood into the barn's framework—an invitation for
> the barn to catch on fire. I yelled and we ran, terrified
> that the barn would go up in smoke and burn quickly—
> killing us and destroying the most important building
> on the farm. From a safe distance away, we watched
> to see if the barn would start glowing with flames.
> Nothing happened. What a relief. The barn was safe
> and we hadn't been caught smoking. We never smoked
> there again.*

We made hay several times in the spring and summer.
The bales had to be lifted from the hayrack onto the elevator
that toted each bale up and dropped it within the waiting
depths. And, of course, it all had to be unloaded and carefully
stacked inside. Someone lifted the heavy bales from the
hayrack onto the elevator. Inside, someone else stacked
bales in tight, neat rows for the best use of space in the barn.

Dad, Ben Kajer and Rose

Before we had the elevator, we used a hay carrier to haul hay into the hayloft. Located at the roof peak of the barn, it ran on a steel track the entire length of the barn. It moved the load by means of a heavy lift rope, one end attached to the load where it ran up to a pulley on the carrier that was directly above the load, then along the track to the far end of the hayloft. Another heavy rope, with another series of pulleys, was attached to the tractor.

Loads of thirty-six to fifty bales were carefully stacked in a rope sling attached to the lift rope. Then the tractor started pulling—moving slowly and carefully away from the barn. The rope grew taut and the sling of bales rose and swung dangerously from side to side. Upon reaching the steel carrier on the track, the carrier abruptly began to move the load horizontally into the barn. This sudden change of direction jerked the load from swaying upwards to swaying sideways.

When the carrier had brought the load to the desired location in the barn, Dad yanked a light trip rope that caused the bales to tumble down to the hayloft floor. Needless to say, Dad had to make sure he was not standing in a spot where a bale might roll onto him. Later, the bales were stacked for storage and packed tightly together in arrow-straight rows that brushed the rafters.

The straw, which was lighter than hay, was stored in the upper loft, and the heavier bales of hay remained on the

9

ground levels. Straw was made from leftovers remaining after the wheat was harvested. The straw was not food, but bedding. Straw absorbed some of the muck, softened the animals' beds and warmed their tired bodies. One of our regular chores was to throw down straw bales and spread the straw in the stalls.

In the middle of the long barn was an open expanse two levels high. At one end of the room were the horse stanchions. On the wall outside the horses' stalls, huge Dutch doors folded down. Through these doors, we pitched hay into the horses' feed bins and straw under their hooves.

To get into the loft, we climbed a ladder built against a wall inside the barn. It led up to the loft through a square opening big enough for us to climb through. It was a bit scary to climb, but we had to go up there to work—and we loved to play up there, too.

The loft was a great place to hang out after harvesting was completed. A long rope dangled from the steel bar that ran the entire length of the barn. We loved to grab the long rope and swing out over the middle section. Whee! We were not supposed to swing from one end of the barn to the other end for fear we would land in the hay bales below and hurt ourselves. Maybe that's what made it even more fun. The scene reminds us of riding a rope from a tall tree over a river and falling into the river below or like a ride in Disneyland. The hay mow was not Disneyland, but it was a great place to work, play, and even hide.

ROSE: *We weren't always playing when we hid. Once, I overheard my parents arguing heatedly— possibly about money and the lack thereof—a common farm problem, especially when the father was spending too much on alcohol. I was terrified. I took Carol and Cathy out of the house to hide in the haymow. Huddling there, I promised myself that I would do my best in school so that I could get a good job, earn money and take them away from the unhappy situation in our home.*

10

In addition to hay, the cattle were also fed silage, which is ground-up, fermented young corn sort of like sauerkraut for cows. The almost-good smell of silage emanated from the silo, which was attached by a chute to the barn. Making silage was a delicate process. Fresh green corn stalks were chopped and blown up into the silo. The corn needed to be ground at a specific stage of maturity and the outdoor temperature needed to be correct for proper fermentation. If overheated, improperly fermented silage caused an unpleasant stench. If all went well, we'd have plenty of good fodder for the cattle to feed on through the winter. When it was processed correctly, it had a distinctive, almost-pleasing odor. (If all went well...)

Of course, we had to work to get the silage back out of the silo to feed to the cattle–rather nasty difficult work. Think of standing ankle-deep in a mixture that's a cross between rotting grass and sauerkraut. Nevertheless, pitching silage was a job we all had to help with. And it wasn't just plain old shoving with the pitch-fork and pitching it down the chute. Dad taught us the correct way to remove silage in the summer to keep a level surface, as we slowly worked down within the silo. We also learned to keep the solid frozen pile level in the winter.

To get into the silo, we had to climb the narrow, slippery, widespread steel rungs attached to the outside of the silo— not something for those with a fear of heights since we went 40-60 feet up. When we reached a square door opening that was about 30 by 30 inches, we crawled into the aromatic and often hot or freezing silo.

When the silage had been removed to a level below the door, Dad climbed up to remove the door so that we could pitch silage down rather than fill a fork and lift it up and out the door. Dad lifted the door up out of the slot, hoisted it above the open space, and slid it into place above our heads.

For a few days we could crawl directly into the silo rather than up and over the space and literally fall into the silo. After pitching silage several days, the level once again

11

required Dad to come up and move the door. All the time the level of silage in the silo was lowered to feed the cows.

> **ROSE:** *Climbing the outside ladder of the silo when it was cold, icy and slippery was difficult. The iron rods were spaced about 20 inches apart. When I entered the silo I would literally fall over the small open door space into the silage. I do not remember having anyone with me. I had to break through the frozen crust of the silage to begin pitching it down. Then I had to carry it out to the individual stalls when I came down from the silo. This was not an easy job for a young girl.*
>
> *Inside, the huge, heavy ten-tine silage fork awaited me. I made the job heavier still by loading the fork as full as possible each time in order to finish the job quickly. (To make the time go faster, I sometimes sang as I worked.)*

In later years, Cathy and Carol—sometimes singing —proceeded to throw enough silage into the annex to feed the cattle.

> **CAROL:** *One time, the tiny confines of the round silo—an area like a Spanish bullfighter's ring—was the scene of a fight. Cathy and I disagreed on some point of discussion. My strongly-voiced opinion did not stand up against Cathy's superior words. To make my point, I aimed my ten-tine fork at her using swear words forbidden to us children. She reciprocated. We caught Dad's attention. He called us down. I went first. He whipped off his belt for my one and only belting. He said, "First come, first served."*

Leaving the silo and its annex, we move into a hallway between the haymow and the milking parlor. Dad had no more than four cows the first few years. The herd gradually increased to ten milk cows. Twice daily, morning and

12

evening, we opened the door for the cattle to enter from the grove. The Holsteins filed into the barn, each going to its own milking stanchion. We walked through the aisle in front of them, closed each stanchion—a sort of large oblong ring around the neck—and then spread silage and hay for them to eat.

The milk bags, or udders, of the cows had to be washed before milking. The four teats on the udder were carefully cleaned and the bags rubbed (or primed) to make the milk flow quickly. Trying to milk a cow as it swished away flies with its dirty tail tried any milker's patience. Keeping the milk clean in an open pail was not an easy task.

> **ROSE:** *Dad teased me by squirting a long stream of milk towards me, trying to hit my open mouth. I tried to avoid this because I was never fond of milk, although I certainly like cream and butter.*

Of course, every farm had cats for keeping down the mice and rats. Farm people thought of them as working animals, not pets. Many of them were half wild. Some were tame enough to be petted. They were mainly females that stayed; the toms usually left when they grew up. Wild or not, most of them still managed to appear when the cows bellowed to be milked. The cats and kittens appeared, waiting for a fresh bowl of warm milk or sometimes a squirt in the mouth that the milker might send their way.

> **CAROL:** *The kittens were my favorite. Mother cats would nest back in little tunnels between bales of hay on the ground floor. Babies. Oh, so soft to touch. I couldn't resist reaching in to try to pet them, but they were wild and scared and batted at me and spat out ferocious hisses, making me jerk my hand back.*
>
> *Mom liked kittens but would not allow pets in the house.*

13

Mom with kitten outside

The corridor led to two doors at the north end of the building. The northeast door was our entrance into the barn to feed the cattle. The cattle also used this as an exit to load the truck at shipping time.

A small room near the silo across the corridor from the cattle provided the space to house sheep or a visiting bull. Our memory of the use of the room includes our one and only pregnant ewe that gave birth to twin lambs. The lambs were quickly moved from the pig house to the warmer small room in the barn. Unfortunately, the ewe rejected her newborn twins: the ewe pushed away her trying-to-nurse youngsters.

To save the lambs, we gathered them in our arms and gently carried them into our warm kitchen. The lambs, with their funny long tails and soft wool made their way into our hearts. Every two hours—just like any baby—we fed them. However, we used tiny doll bottles to feed them.

Kept very warm in a box behind the wood stove, they grew bigger and bigger until they drank from regular baby bottles. After smelling lamb's wool in the kitchen for one season, Mom may have convinced Dad to no longer raise lambs.

The room in the barn where the lambs were supposed to be with their mother, was off-limits periodically when a bull was brought over from another farm to breed the cows. The bull was usually kept in this room of the barn near the silo to be secluded from the cows. The visiting bull stayed at our farm only briefly. As soon as possible he was shipped back to its owner since we didn't want to have to deal with this huge, dangerous, and often ill-tempered fellow any longer than necessary.

The small room housed the sheep or bull at one end of the barn. At the other end of the building, horses were stabled. We had three horses: the team of Tom and Jerry—huge, mean, kicking, teeth-baring broncos that frightened us—and the gentle mare Queenie.

Before Dad purchased a tractor, the horses moved the farm's equipment, wagons, and machinery to till the fields of grain, corn, and hay. The horses walked through the pasture outside their stabled area of the barn.

An area of pasture surrounded by the watering tank, milk house, and garage ended at the property line near the silo. The fence ran from the people's entrance of the barn to the watering tank, turned east to the milk house, then began again on the milk house's opposite side. There, a small wooden gate allowed single persons to enter the pasture. Next to it, a large swinging gate, also painted white, allowed a team of horses to enter or exit, a truck to enter to load cattle, or a rack to deliver loads of hay or straw. The fence continued at the kitty-corner end of the garage and ended at the property-line fence.

Gates to Barn

15

Inside the barn, Dad hitched the team together with a heavy wooden yoke and leather straps. He led them through the pasture and through the wide swinging gate between the garage and milk house to the farm machine to be used that day.

In going to the fields, Dad led the team past the milk house and granary, down the lane past the corncrib and chicken house, and through the shaded area of trees that served as a winter windbreak. At last, field work with horse-drawn equipment could begin.

The driveway circle in front of the garage, milk house, and house also led to the highway. Dad often exchanged help with neighbors at planting or harvest time. To help these neighbors, Dad used the circular drive to reach the highway leading to neighboring farms.

On one occasion, Dad told of driving the team to the farm across the road when a semi-truck sped along blowing its horn and frightening the team. Of course, they bolted, turned and headed back toward home and nearly threw Dad from the hay rack. It is not unusual for frightened horses to bolt and run for home. When frightened, nothing could stop them. Dad suffered injuries.

Queenie and Jerry till the garden

CAROL: *Dad told us, "Something spooked Tom and Jerry when driving them along the highway. The*

16

*rollover left me with scars on my legs." Sometime
after that runaway, Dad sold the horses. We were not
sorry to have the team replaced by a tractor.*

Queenie was a very gentle, calm old white mare. Her
job was to slowly pull the plow to till the garden near the
yard. But we were more interested in the occasional rides on
Queenie. Dad trusted her to give us a safe, slow ride.

Cathy, Carol and Rose on Queenie

ROSE: *One hot summer day, Queenie was grazing
in the field near a barbed-wire fence. A severe thunder
storm suddenly developed. Poor Queenie was struck
and killed by lightning. She lay there dead, her legs
sticking straight into the air. Seeing the upended dead
horse, so beloved to me as a small girl, is a picture
embedded deep in my mind. As so often occurs, the
sun shines brightly after a huge lightening storm. The
day was beautiful, but I have never forgotten the sight
of the dead animal bloated with legs pointing upright.
It was not a pretty sight but a memorable lesson about
the cycle of life. The rendering company was called to
remove the carcass.*

After doing chores, cleaning the barn was next. The barn
contained lots of manure. Horse manure had straw mixed in
and we pitched it out the door. We pitched manure out the

window behind the cow stanchions. The cow manure was soft, warm, and smelly.

Later, we hauled manure to the fields. Sometimes we couldn't haul it. If the snow was deep for weeks on end, the manure piles from the cows and the horses stacked up. Then we waited for spring to load, haul, and spread the manure in the fields.

While loading manure in the spring when the pile was warm with fermentation, we chose to go barefoot rather than wear shoes. If we wore shoes in the manure pile, the shoes needed airing and cleaning before we could wear them to school. Yes, we had a total of three pairs of shoes — one for church, one for school, and possibly one too-small pair to use for farm work. To protect our shoes, we had two pairs of overshoes — black buckled overshoes and light brown pull-on overshoes. The black buckled boots were work boots while the light brown ones were more of a fashion statement for girls when attending church or school. Remember, there was always snow or mud to contend with.

We were not afraid to work or play in muck. We went barefoot in the barnyard and cooled our feet in the slough where cattle also cooled themselves in the shallow water standing in the field.

> **ROSE:** *No city pool or chlorine water for us. One unexpected thing happened while walking barefoot in the manure pile. A loose board had been tossed into the pile with a nail protruding. I stepped on that nail and punctured my foot. We did not visit the doctor. The usual remedy included ample bleeding followed by a salt-water soaking. I don't know whether I received a tetanus shot earlier in my life to prevent a bacterial infection. I do know my foot was sore for a few days.*

There was a saying that children needed to eat a bushel of dirt before they grew up. It does seem that kids on the farm developed immunity to many things. How this contrasts with the present notion that everything, especially hands, must be scrubbed and sanitized. There is some benefit to being exposed to little bits of bacteria as one grows up.

THE MILK HOUSE

As one drives into the farm, one can see a tiny building at left center stage: our milk house. Like most farmers of that time, Dad had some dairy cows. To keep cows, you need a milk house. Dad envisioned, designed and built ours in 1936. A white building with doors opening to the east and west, it was sometimes a bit breezy. Windows on the north and south provided light before electricity. This tiny building still exists.

The milk house seems very small today. But back then, we kept just a few cows, about what every farm family had. Cows were milked twice daily in the barn. The cows were pastured between milking, morning and evening. To increase production, cows are now milked three times a day. Between the two milkings, we cleaned away the cow pies, pitched out the manure, and spread clean straw to prepare for milking.

After milking, we carried the milk from the barn to the milk house where the separator removed the cream from the milk. Then the milk went into the cold water tank in five gallon milk cans. Cleaning the separator with cold water was a daily chore whether in freezing cold or muggy hot weather. Hot water was not used on the separator. In the one-room milkhouse was a furnace with a reservoir above it. The furnace heated water for cleaning and sterilizing the milk equipment.

The milk house stands above a well. Water was needed to wash the cows' udders as well as to water the cows. We also stood the big metal cans of milk in the very cold water in the water tank to cool and keep the milk. All farmers did this before the days of electricity and refrigeration.

A tall hand pump stood above the well. A short hose from the pump filled the water tank used to store the milk. When the hose was dropped, the cold water trickled from the water pump hose to cool the milk house floor and our bare feet on hot summer days. A drain hole emptied water into the pasture south of the milk house.

Water from the water tank was piped to a large watering trough situated at the end of a fence that separated the horses from the cattle. Animals could drink from either end of the trough.

Naturally, some youngsters had other ideas for the use of the watering trough. One steamy summer afternoon, we girls floated an over-sized cucumber in the tank. We scooped out the innards and the shell of the cucumber glided like a perfect little canoe. Sometimes we climbed into the water tank to swim—definitely a cooling dunk for a youngster. Carol remembers a cousin showed us how to hold a cat by the tail and dunk the poor thing in the cow tank. The cat wasn't too happy—but it lived.

The water tank was an important spot in the milk house. During hot summer months, Dad chilled his beer in the cement water tank. Quickly, the beer disappeared as Dad drank bottle after bottle. Then, the emptied bottles were stacked in the northwest corner of the milk house. How many cases? Seven or eight. He got refills when the cases were empty.

When the long, rectangular furnace, with a like-sized covered reservoir on top, was no longer needed for cleaning the milk cans, Dad had another reason for heating the water.

CAROL: *Dad continued stoking the bottom portion of the furnace with firewood to heat water in the* *upper portion. He claimed that the warm water in the reservoir of the furnace was good for the pigs. However, more than once I observed him dunk his arm down into the reservoir, pull up a pint, take a swig and then gulp a hefty chaser of beer.*

The cold water tank kept milk fresh until transported to the creamery. We usually filled several cans before a run to the creamery every two or three days. So our milk house was ample for our needs.

Dad delivered and sold our cream and milk to the Steele Center Creamery. Steele Center, about two miles south of our farm, grew with the addition of a grocery store, a repair garage and a gas station across the road from the creamery. Steele Center was a place where Dad shopped for groceries at the convenience store and bought gas for the truck. If allowed to accompany him, Rose remembers she received a special treat of a five-cent double-dipped ice cream cone.

Steele Center Creamery received about 15,000 pounds of milk per day in 1893. Butter was produced and shipped by rail to New York. Butter production peaked in 1942 with 283,525 pounds of butter produced.

Long before automobiles, small township meeting halls were established every few miles to accommodate local farmers who could reach the creamery and tiny grocery store by horse. Somerset Town Hall—formerly a German Lutheran Church—located a quarter mile north of Steele Center became a community meeting center. Impromptu socials with food and music took place after a business meeting.

Mom's brothers were adept at playing several instruments, including the fiddle or violin, drums, saxophone, trombone, and accordion. They were easy to carry along. Perhaps one or other of these instruments was preferred (just as today's youth prefer the guitar).

An impromptu group of musicians could easily set up at the town hall and provide music for a dance. Mom and Dad attended the dances when her brothers played, and they met at one of these local dances, probably at Auditorium Hall in Owatonna.

Today's dairy farms have huge barns where dozens and dozens of cows are milked by electric milking machines with 'fingers' that attach to each of the cow's teats. The milk is transferred directly to a bulk machine. Not back then. Milking was done by hand, carried to the milk house by hand, separated and cooled in a cold water tank and finally transferred to the creamery to sell. It was hard work.

Dad used a milk machine only a few years before selling the dairy cattle. While milking cows was profitable, Dad had troubles with his back and decided to raise Herefords rather than milk cows. However, he did keep one milk cow, Bessie, a very gentle roan-colored milking cow to supply our milk and cream. Later, when the horses and cows were sold, Bessie, our one milk cow, took over the horse barn.

> **ROSE:** *Bessie was kept in the now-empty room where the horses had been. I was still quite young, maybe twelve, when Dad decided it was time for me to learn how to milk a cow by hand. Dad placed the small stool beside the cow and I squatted on the three-legged stool, my head against the belly of the cow and placed my hands around two of the four teats and began to pull. There is some technique to milking that is a combination of squeeze and pull to release the milk.*
>
> *It seems this technique was beyond my capability. Try as I might, I could never get more than an inch of milk in the pail. Bessie was such an easy milker, meaning she almost let the milk down without any pull and Dad could easily fill a pail with rich frothy warm milk in two minutes. He had me try several days but with much consternation decided that I would never be a milkmaid. Thus my milking career ended.*

Two milkings a day provided more milk and cream than

could be used in one day, but too little to separate to sell—so, a cream separator was no longer needed.

The thick rich cream that rose to the top was perfect for making butter, ice cream, and other rich desserts. Before we had only one milk cow, the cream was poured into a container directly from the cream can. Now after milking, rich cream was skimmed from the top of the milk.

We had to purchase a small glass butter maker so that we could churn our own butter. We sat on the floor in the kitchen to churn the cream in a gallon jar with paddles attached to the inside of the cover. When we turned the handle, the four paddles lapped at the cream until the cream coagulated. Mother salted it, added food coloring to make it yellow, and placed the round ball on a plate in the refrigerator for later use. We loved to slather this rich butter on garden-grown hot corn-on-the-cob.

When Dad's back problem made raising dairy cattle 24/7 too difficult, he slowly switched to raising beef cattle. Beef cattle (Herefords on our farm), steers (raised to sell), cows and calves were pastured near the barn in a grove of trees west of the barn. This area was fenced to keep cows out of the fields beyond the grove. There, they grazed on grassy spots in the wooded area, or lying down, slowly chewed their cud.

Unlike bulls, cows are usually placid, but they, too, can be dangerous—especially if they think their calves are being threatened—and even more so if the calf is just a new-born. The Herefords, which were domesticated but not really tame, tended to be more prone to charging us since they didn't have the close, twice-daily interaction with us during milking that the dairy cows did. Regardless of breed or sex, they were huge animals: just getting stepped on could break a foot. And, the cows weren't particularly concerned about whether they were squeezing us against a wall.

Rose had a couple of scares with the Herefords. Once a Hereford cow calved in an open area of the barn. Dad told Rose to walk slowly against the far wall past the cow to feed the horses beyond. The cow didn't know Rose meant no harm to her new-born baby and butted Rose against the wall. Dad quickly grabbed a haying four-tine pitchfork and poked the angry cow away.

> **ROSE:** *One winter morning, when the Herefords were wandering to the west of the barn on a winter morning, Dad was separating the steers for sale. We were in the snowy, icy grove of trees. I was driving the steers toward the gate when a mother cow saw me approach. Her calf was not far from me and the cow thought I was about to harm her calf. She ran towards me. In fear and panic, I ran and ducked around a tree trying to hide from the cow. I slipped and fell on an icy patch at the foot of the tree. It so startled the cow that she turned and ran. Hilarious to observe—but frightening.*

Dad was proud of his Hereford cattle and encouraged Rose, Carol and Cathy to take the 4-H cattle project, which gave farm kids experience raising their own cows or steers. The animals were shown at the county fair for prizes, then auctioned off.

> **ROSE:** *I showed a steer at the Steele County Fair two years. I loved my first one, which I named Buster. I fed, groomed, petted, and talked to him to tame him so he would show well at the fair. I was supposed to halter-train him so he could be walked in the show ring at the fair, but I didn't try until early summer. By that time, he was nearing nine months old and would soon weigh 1000 pounds—far too big for me to simply pull him around by myself. So we used a training shortcut. We hooked his halter to a rope attached to the tractor. Then, I drove the tractor slowly around and around our circular driveway until Buster got the idea of moving where the rope tugged him. Soon I could lead him without the tractor.*

Rose leading Buster

I put a lot into raising and training Buster, so there were some tears and hesitation when the time came for him to be auctioned off after the judging at the fair. I loved my second steer, Buster II, as well. He placed last in the judging but was sold for the record-high price per pound at the auction. The going price per pound at the auction that day was twenty-three cents. I received forty-one cents per pound. I was somewhat sad again at the sale of my 1,000 pound pet steer but delighted to get all that money to put into my college fund.

After harvest, we released the Herefords into the fenced-off cornfields to glean the dropped corn and eat some of the cornstalks. One sunny fall day, Cousin Mary Lou was visiting.

CAROL: *Dad asked Mary Lou and me to take the truck to the corn field, chop corn stalks and load the stalks onto the pick-up, then unload them in the field for the cows. I was just learning to drive the pick-up. Upon reaching the hill, Mary Lou suggested, "You drive the pick-up over that hill and as you do that, I'll pull off the corn stalks."*

26

After three starts and stalls, Mary Lou—standing behind the truck waiting for action—yelled, "Gun 'er, Carol." I followed instructions, leaving Mary Lou standing with the corn stalks on the back side of the hill.

The purpose of our milk house changed with the decision to no longer keep dairy cattle. It became Dad's office. A business desk replaced the cream separator after the addition of electricity. In the southeast corner, Dad's drop-leaf desk stored all kinds of important things in its various cubby holes. Yearly, he kept meticulous farm records: a diary of daily weather conditions, the date he planted corn, wheat and other crops, harvest yields, cost of purchased equipment, and market yields on pigs or Hereford cows. A small electric heater stood beside the desk and provided year-round comfort in the milk house.

Grandson Larry with Grandpa Lawrence

CAROL: *This desk also held a variety of Dad's special collections: cigarettes, pipes, and cigars. Cathy and I made sure we tried each of these tasty (cough, cough) treasures. We'd sneak to a location where no one would suspect us of smoking—up in the barn, behind an old shack on the way to the fields, but never in the milk house.*

Special "recipes" were among his collections. He kept

27

these as reminders of ways to live one's life and love others. "Plant Happiness" is one example:

First, plant five rows of peas: Prayer, Perseverance, Politeness, Promptness, Purity. Next, plant three rows of squash: Squash gossip. Squash doubt. Squash indifference. Then, five rows of lettuce: Let us be faithful to duty. Let us be unselfish. Let us be gentle. Let us follow wisdom. Let us love life. No garden is complete without turnips: Turn up for church. Turn up with a smile. Turn up with new ideas. Turn up with determination to make everything count for something good and worthwhile.

"Recipe for a Happy New Year" is another example:

Take twelve whole months. Clean them thoroughly of all bitterness, hate, and jealousy. Make them just as fresh and clean as possible. Now cut each month into twenty-eight, thirty, or thirty-one different parts—but don't make up the whole batch at once. Prepare it one day at a time out of these ingredients. Mix well into each day one part of faith, one part of patience, one part of courage, and one part of work. Add to each day one part of hope, faithfulness, generosity, and kindness. Blend with one part prayer, one part meditation, and one good deed. Season the whole with a dash of good spirits, a sprinkle of fun, a pinch of play, and a cupful of good humor. Pour all of this into a vessel of love. Cook thoroughly over radiant joy, garnish with a smile, and serve with quietness, unselfishness, and cheerfulness. You're bound to have a happy new year.

Mom and Dad followed the golden rule and taught us that "If you can't say something good about someone, don't say anything at all." They really lived that adage themselves. Through another saying, "Something good can be found in everyone," we learned that God can be found in everyone.

The milk house, as his business office, was the hub of Dad's operations, linking all other buildings on the farm. There were several well-worn paths leading out from it to other parts of the farm. While the milk house continues to stand in 2012 at the center of the farm, other buildings have been removed, and the house has been remodeled and extended. We wonder about its use in today's world.

> **ROSE:** *Today, we might call the milk house a man cave because it became a place for guys to visit, have a beer, and play cards. Or it might be the forerunner of the water cooler as a place to take a break, greet your fellow workers, or gossip a bit before returning to work.*

CHICKEN HOUSES

Early in their marriage, Dad and Mom housed about 30 laying hens and five roosters in a small room of the barn. The hens provided both eggs and meat for the family. During the cold winter months, Mom was lucky to pick six or eight eggs a day because hens do not lay an egg every day. But six eggs a day were more than enough for the family needs.

In the winter of 1937, the extra eggs that had accumulated over the months fed a very large group of unexpected overnight guests who'd been stranded by the snow.

Snow on the highway had always been a problem on our stretch of the highway. The woods surrounding our house, situated on a slight rise of land, protected our home from the blowing winds. But the blowing snow across the open highway north of our house soon covered the highway with deep solid snow banks that slowed down and sometimes completely stopped traffic. Dad put up six-foot snow fences to the north of our woods. This stopped the drifting snow at the line of the fence so that it did not cross the highway. Prior to that, there was havoc on the highway those first winters our parents were on the farm.

Where our property ended on the south end of the farmstead, there was no snow fence. In addition to drifting snow, the cars now encountered one of the few hills in this part of Minnesota. Here the drifting snow eventually reached a height of six or more feet. This is when trouble began.

A semi-truck attempted to climb the slight hill. Slipping and sliding on the snow-covered road, the truck slowed. Soon another truck approached, slowed into a slide and jackknifed, closing the highway. Although some cars made it around the first semi, others were blocked by the snow which continued to drift. Telephone lines were down and snowplows couldn't reach the stranded cars. The roads became more slippery and snowdrifts deeper as the evening went on. The first truck stalled around nine o'clock in the evening. The second semi completely blocked the road. One car after another also stalled. No one could turn around.

At about eleven o'clock, Dad went out to view the situation. He realized the danger of a night in the car, so he invited the folks from the two trucks and five cars to come into the house for warmth and safety from the howling blizzard. There were about fifteen unexpected guests to feed and house that night.

Because hospitality—offering coffee and food—was a tradition in farm homes, Mom faced a dilemma. *What could she serve so many unexpected, unhappy, hungry guests?* Then the driver of a stranded bread truck offered Mom bread from his truck. And of course, she had plenty of eggs. Voila! A much-appreciated meal: eggs, bread and milk. Yes, bread and eggs fed the crowd. While some helped prepare food, others gathered rugs and blankets to sleep on the living room rug. A snowplow came the next morning to plow open the road. The people were on their way.

Our family used eggs in many ways for cooking, baking, and making desserts in addition to selling them. We served the following favorite dessert recipe in the winter when eggs and milk were plentiful.

Graham Cracker Pudding:

Crush 12 double graham crackers. Add 1/3 C. granulated sugar and ½ C. melted butter.

31

Place half of the crumbs on the bottom of 8" square baking dish. Reserve half of the crumbs for topping over custard.

Custard: Whisk together ¾ C. sugar, 2 T. cornstarch, ½ tsp. salt.

Then whisk in a 2 qt. saucepan: 2 egg yolks and 2 C. milk. Continue to whisk and cook until thickened. Stir in 1 tsp. vanilla. Pour over crumbs.

Beat 2 egg whites stiff. Add ¼ tsp. cream of tartar and 2 T. sugar. Spread egg whites on custard. Sprinkle remaining crumbs on top. Bake in 300° oven for 30 minutes. Chill.

The aroma of Mom's desserts and her fried-chicken dinners are permanently stamped in our memories. Folks in town also had a desire for spring fryers. So Dad saw another avenue for more income and decided to raise young cockerels—another name for young roosters—to sell as dressed spring fryers. He knew that people in town would appreciate farm-fresh chickens. He chose Rhode Island Red roosters (no hens) because they grew quickly—in ten short weeks—to plump young three-pound fryers. He knew we could butcher, dress, and sell them as farm-fresh fryers.

Early each April (for about three years in the 1950s), he purchased 250 day-old chicks. A very small brooder house was pulled into the apple orchard and the short three-month growing season for the fryers began. Looking at pictures, we noticed that the small brooder house was moved to several different locations over the years. In one photo it is located behind the granary. In another, the brooder house is near the corncrib. At other times it sat on two different sides of the barn. We remember it sitting in the apple orchard awaiting the arrival of the baby chicks.

Dad did not want the brooder house on the front lawn during off-seasons, but it's a puzzle why he moved it to different locations. One could guess the brooder house was moved to a new location to house baby pigs, and another place to store shelled corn, and possibly a third place to simply keep it out of sight until the arrival of next year's chicks.

Chicks were hatched somewhere—we knew not where—and could be ordered by mail. The day-old chicks were transported in flats about four inches high. Dad would drive into town to pick them up at the post office. We moved the flats from Dad's truck bed into their new home, the brooder house. The soft, warm chicks were carefully lifted one by one and spaced around the room.

The brooder house was a single room with windows to provide light. A large heat lamp in the center warmed the room and protected the chicks from the early spring chill. Wire mesh surrounded the heating unit to keep the chicks a safe distance from the bulb.

New chicks required a temperature of 90 to 95 degrees upon arrival. The temperature was reduced about five degrees each week for the next five weeks. After five weeks, no supplemental heat was needed unless outdoor temperatures came close to freezing or below. If the chicks were seen crowding tightly and piling onto each other, we had a clue that they were cold. When they avoided the heated area, we knew they were too warm.

Several other measures were taken to keep the delicate young chicks alive and healthy. Immediately upon arrival, chicks required room-temperature water served in a drown-proof watering container. Feeders designed to prevent grain from being scratched out helped reduce the amount of wasted feed.

As the spring days grew warmer and the chicks grew bigger, we let them outside. A trap door close to the floor opened to an east-facing fenced area for the chicks to enjoy the out-of-doors. The birds scampered from the ramp to the grassy area to scratch the ground for angle worms or other enticing tidbits. The chicks grew rapidly; the soft fuzz soon turned to feathers.

CAROL: *The chicks were so cute and a feast for the senses. They made cheery little "cheep, cheep, cheeps" and their soft, fluffy fuzz tickled our cheeks. Their antics were fun to watch. Whenever I got the blues, just standing and watching them brought me peace and laughter. The brooder house was a healing haven.*

Selling spring fryers was an excellent money-making project, but it meant hard work for Mom and us girls. Dad planned the project, oversaw the raising of the chicks, and then advertised – fresh farm fryers for sale.

Starting in mid-July, we slaughtered and dressed out chickens once a week. It was a big production. Dad started the butchering process and killed the chickens for the day's sale. However, dressing them—stripping the feathers, picking pin-feathers, gutting the chickens—and wrapping them for sale was women's work.

Preparing about thirty spring fryers for sale in one day required an assembly line. Dad was the first and his job was to kill the chicken. The bird was placed on top of a large flat stump. Dad, with his foot on top of the bird's head, used an axe to sever the chicken's head from its body. As he threw it from him to avoid the spurting blood, we watched it flop down the grassy hillside west of the house. We had a very clear picture of what was meant by "running around like a chicken with its head cut off." Kicking out with jerky legs, flopping up and down, and spurting blood from their headless necks offered a gruesome sight.

Once they stopped flopping, we gathered them and took them into the house. Mom boiled water on the gas stove in a long deep boiler that covered two burners. Into this receptacle she dunked the chicken (a stinky job), which loosened the feathers enough to be pulled from the body. Mom then brought the bird to the kitchen table and plucked its feathers. She handed the chicken to Rose for gutting.

34

Finally, the bird was passed to Carol or Cathy for picking off the pin-feathers. The chickens were chilled in cold water in the bathtub. Running water from spigots made cooling the birds easy.

Chicken orders were prepared for pick-up on Friday or Saturday. We often prepared thirty to forty chickens a weekend. Dad advertised in the newspaper each week and took orders over the phone. Mom would carefully wrap the fresh fryers in freezer paper and then Dad delivered them to some customers.

> **ROSE:** *Today, I would never choose to kill, clean and dress a chicken, but I certainly can cut up a whole fryer with skill and ease. I appreciate that I can readily purchase a whole fryer in the supermarket. However, no supermarket chicken can compete with the flavor of a farm-fresh fryer.*

After a couple of years, Dad built a large two-story chicken house to raise laying hens. He had switched from raising cockerels (roosters) to raising pullets (laying hens). Pullets needed to be treated for internal and external parasites such as lice, mites and fleas. Dad held the chicken's mouth open by pulling on the top and bottom combs while one of us girls poked a pill down its throat with an index finger. Pesky job, but someone had to do it.

The chicken house was built far from the house and close to the granary. In the morning and evening chicken feed was carried from the granary to the chicken house. Eggs were gathered once a day. The chicken house was cleaned once a week.

> **ROSE:** *Early one Saturday morning Dad called sharply up the stairway (he was very unhappy that I was not up) to tell me to get right downstairs and get out and do my chores. It was Saturday morning—time to clean the chicken house. I was in tenth grade and*

in bed with a high fever and chicken pox all over my body. I refused and he relented.

There were many chicken house-cleaning Saturdays in store for us. The reward for removing chicken manure was the chance to go to the upper story of this new building and throw down the clean, golden straw which would be the new bedding for the chickens.

Covering all but the feeding area, a large square wooden platform with attached wire mesh about twelve inches above it hung in the center of the hen house. Wooden bars ranged at regular intervals above the mesh so that the chickens could roost there when not feeding or ambling around on the floor. The platform below the roosting area caught the chickens' excreted waste.

CAROL: *On one occasion, a rooster, roosting on the bars above the platform, eyed me. He jumped at me and clawed my head with his sharp talons. Blood ran down my nose and drip, drip, dripped. I ran into the house. By the time I got there, I thought I was dying because there was now a profuse amount of blood coming out of my head. But Mother told me that any head wound bleeds a lot, and mine was really just minor. She cleaned it. That—and all the blood flushing the cut—cleaned away any germs that might otherwise have tried to get in.*

Someone had to clean the platform on a regular basis. The chickens were shooed into a fenced area during the cleaning spree. The mesh and the bar area tilted up and hooked in place so we could rake the droppings off the platform. Most droppings were well dried by this time.

Cathy and Carol were eventually promoted to the task of throwing the manure outside to the east and loading it into the manure spreader before taking it to the field for spreading.

CAROL: *One winter day when we were not using the*

manure spreader for its usual use, a bunch of us kids—
some cousins were with us—piled into the spreader,
which was hooked to the tractor, and went out to the
field to ski. Ropes tied to the spreader pulled the skiers
along with ease over the freshly fallen inches of snow.
We were having great fun until Cathy wanted to take
my place as driver. I did not wish to give up the throne,
so I elbowed her. She fell beneath the wheels of the
spreader. Chagrinned, I jumped down to see if she was
still alive. Because the spreader was empty, no damage
was done. What a relief. So we continued skiing.

After cleaning away the smelly manure from the floor and platform, straw was spread over the platform to catch and absorb future chicken droppings. This straw was stored in the second story.

Carol remembers the hen house had a north-facing door on the second story. Getting to the second story wasn't exactly easy or fun, however. The door swung outward and could be reached only by climbing a ladder braced against the outside of the building. She climbed the wobbly ladder, reached over to her right to swing open the door, and climbed over into the opening from the ladder. Fear of falling gripped her each time she needed to climb it. Some years later, during her late teens, Dad built an outdoor stairway to a second-story door on the opposite end of the hen house.

In the ceiling of the lower level, a hole on the northwestern corner opened into the second story. There was no ladder built onto the wall here because the chickens would have used it as a roosting place. Yuck.

When we were upstairs, we opened the trap door, removed the twine from the bales and dropped loose straw onto the floor below. Most straw was scattered onto the floor and some on the platform to replace the droppings, now called straw manure, which had been removed earlier.

After cleaning the chicken house, Rose drove the tractor—pulling the spreader—to fertilize the fields with the chicken manure. While this sounds like an unpleasant task, the times spent in the field were actually times of peace and quiet.

By the time she was a high school senior, Rose had acquired much tractor knowledge. She put it to use when she entered the Queen of the Furrow contest.

> **ROSE:** *The written test covered questions about soil conservation, crop rotation, water and land usage. I competed with girls from the state at the event named "Plowville" in Renville, Minnesota. My test score plus tractor driving skills earned second place for me at the state competition.*
>
> *Driving a similar tractor—but not Dad's tractor—I pulled a long empty hay wagon through a series of orange cones that looked like a slalom ski course. We never had orange cones in our fields, and, sadly, the rear edge of the wagon knocked over the first cone and continued to knock over each following cone on the course. Oh well, second place at the state level was not too bad.*

Cleaning the chicken house kept the chickens' feet cleaner. Eggs were also cleaner and picking the eggs was then not such a dirty job. Along three of the walls, Dad built a series of joined-together wooden boxes with holes large enough for the hens to enter. We stuffed straw into the boxes. Sometimes when our gathering began, hens were sitting on the nest. Usually they simply jumped from the nest when a hand came near the hole. Other times they struck out with their sharp beaks. Ouch. Fear, begone! Sometimes a chicken excreted its sticky, smelly droppings into the nest before laying the egg. Then the egg was encrusted with the droppings. Disgusting.

The eggs were carefully cleaned and packed to receive the highest egg price of the day. Before packing them, we carefully checked for cracks or dirty spots. Washing off

38

dirty eggs was a smelly job. Eggs were washed quickly because the shells can be permeated by water and eventually even discolored if chicken droppings adhere. The eggs were packed carefully into cases that held twelve dozen eggs.

> **CAROL:** *Cousin Dick told about finding coins at the bottom of his pail—his Dad's way of encouraging the kids to CHOOSE to pack eggs. Sadly, our wire baskets did not contain coins; they would have disappeared between the heavy-duty wires of the basket.*

The egg cases were stored in the basement until we had several cases filled and ready to deliver and sell to Kelly's Department Store. At the store, Carol remembers observing the candling process. Candling of eggs was done by hand. One time Mom's cousin, a Kelly's employee, took Carol to the basement where he showed her how he culled eggs to see whether they were ready or not for sale.

To start candling eggs, an egg was picked up lengthways between his forefinger and thumb and held directly up to the light exit hole in the candler. This ray of light was focused through a hole in the box. The light showed the inside of the egg. The egg was visually inspected to check the development and integrity of each egg. He examined the egg to see whether it was fresh and infertile, addled or fertile. He looked for fresh and infertile eggs, ones that would be used for sale. Addled, decomposing fertile eggs—which looked cloudy, spotted or had irregular lines at the sides—and fertile eggs—which showed an embryo developing (a dark body with radiating spider-like blood vessels)—were not sold by Kelly's.

Rose recalls other departments of the store. She enjoyed Saturday trips to town when Dad hauled eggs to sell at Kelly's Department Store. We entered at the back entrance of Kelly's, also the hardware and feed store section of the store. There the eggs were candled in the basement of the store. Dad was credited with the market value of the eggs that day. We would walk past the hardware items and into the grocery section. Oh, the bananas and oranges looked good. Living on a farm we needed to buy only a few groceries, such as flour and sugar. The total cost of our items was subtracted from the credit we received for our sale of eggs. The store kept a running summary of our account and we could purchase items throughout the store. Hardware, clothing, shoes and many other items were purchased at Kelly's Department Store. The clothing section was the girls' favorite part of the store.

> **ROSE:** *I think of Kelly's as an early version of a Target Super Store. If time allowed, I could wander through the store—first the fabric and household items, and all the way through to the beautiful women's section at the far end of the building. Most women chose to enter the store from the clothing side of the building.*

Around the corner was a jewelry store and across one more street the Dime Store. Yes, we had a five- and ten-cent store long before the Dollar Store. But to the left of Kelly's Department Store was Hoff's Bar where Dad spent his time while we were looking at clothing.

Shoppers and visitors alike could stop at Central Park on Saturday evening to hear the band play and catch up on news of the day or week. Saturday evening gatherings at Central Park featured Owatonna's own band. The bandstand, located in the middle of the center-piece block, was surrounded by people seated on folding chairs or milling around the area. Some people even went across the street from Central Park to Gordon's, the place to stop for an ice cream treat.

The bandstand was built before 1897 and was torn down in 1976. Les Abraham was commissioned to design the new bandstand, which was completed in 2004. The bandstand of 2004 looks familiar although the new design features a whole side that unfolds to make a complete stage.

Central Park Bandstand

On another corner from the bandstand we banked at First National Bank designed by Frank Lloyd Wright. Today it is on the National Register of Historic Places.

THE GARAGE

Our garage was built primarily for keeping the car from being buried in snow in the long cold Minnesota winters. Snow banks in the yard were often six to eight feet deep. Only the car was stored in the garage; the farm machinery spent the winter in sheds.

The first car to be parked in the garage, a new black 1936 Dodge pick-up truck, was used on the farm for the next twenty years. It was a wedding gift from Grandpa and Grandma Deml. Dad's shiny new truck may have been the result of the earlier monetary deprivation in his youth.

As a teenager, whenever Dad made money working on other farms, Grandpa exacted the money from him—a practice Dad did not appreciate, although it was common for teenage farm children to contribute to the family's finances. He learned—years later—that Grandpa had set aside Dad's money for future use by Dad.

At the time Dad purchased the farm, Grandpa and Grandma helped him get started not only by holding the mortgage but also by giving him a few cows, pigs, and chickens.

That truck with its narrow bench seat, was the only vehicle we had to drive us to town, to church, or to visit relatives. Dad, Mom, Rose, Carol, and Cathy each had a very specific place to sit. We crowded in and straddled the stick-shift transmission located in the center of the floor board.

CAROL: *I was five or six years old when we piled into the truck to go to Uncle Edward's place for a Christmas Eve celebration. Dad drove. Cathy, about age three, sat on Mom's lap. Rose, about nine years old, sat in the middle with me on her lap. When Dad was about to change gears, he'd say, "Ready?" Then he moved the stick shift on the floor from second into high gear. Bang, it went right down between our legs and there it stayed until the next stop sign. Thankfully, there were no stop signs on the eight-mile ride to Uncle Edward's farm.*

The garage changed very little over the years, but there was a progression of cars and machinery in front of it. A horse-drawn, one-bottom plow was replaced with a two-bottom plow and tractor. A community-shared threshing machine was no longer needed after Dad purchased a grain combine and started doing custom work for the neighbors. Dad also purchased a John Deere wire hay baler—extremely innovative at the time—for his custom work.

The garage was, however, also Dad's workshop and the place where he kept his tools and lots of supplies and odds and ends that might be used for repairs or building.

The garage also served as a machine shop. Frequently, a piece of machinery was in need of repair. A farmer had to be a repairman and inventor to keep things working. The garage stored treasures of fascinating items—purchased or saved—to fix anything and everything.

In the rush of meeting farm deadlines—planting and harvesting crops—the garage's workbench became totally disorganized. Cleaning the garage meant sorting tools, rearranging items and discovering unexpected storage space for things that might be useful in the future. We saved items for future use—much as people store extras in attics today.

The garage was the place to find farmers inspecting and readying machinery for planting. The grain seeder and tractor were the first to be oiled and greased; bolts were tightened and given a very careful inspection to check that the machine was safe for use.

ROSE: *As Dad's number-one helper outside (there were no boys in our family), I learned to grease farm machinery, search for the tools that might be needed while out working in the fields, and fill the tractor with gas. Life, cars and machinery have become more complex since then. Now, I no longer put gas in the car or even change a light bulb in the house.*

After electricity was installed on the farm, the garage had more light, but, as was typical of the time, it was only a single light bulb hanging from the center of the room—not over the workbench. Still with that one light bulb, Dad had enough light to use his workbench any time of the day.

Originally, daylight provided the only light in the garage. The garage doors swung out wide enough for one vehicle to enter and, if open during the day, provided light. Two narrow windows near the roof line shed some light over the long workbench on the east wall.

Electricity came to the countryside as a result of President Roosevelt's 1935 order implementing an emergency program to provide electricity to farms (the Rural Electrification Act, or REA). The next year, Congress supported Roosevelt's order and electricity for farms was assured. Mom and Dad were married the next year. However, five years went by before electricity came to our rural area.

CAROL: *How grateful Mom and Dad must have been to have electricity. I am amazed when I consider the major differences of their growing-up years on a farm compared with mine, simply due to lack of electricity. I can only imagine the brightness of the rooms and lightness of heart electricity must have brought to country people. Although I do not remember kerosene lamps, Mom talked about what a mess it was to clean them. Two of our kerosene lamps were converted to electric table lamps. Change was coming to the farm.*

The garage housed screens in the winter, storm windows in the summer. In the spring, all storm windows were removed from the house and screens replaced them. Winter frosts and thaws loosened putty that secured the frame around the glass of the windows. Dad placed these windows on two sawhorses found in the garage. Old dried dull paint was scraped off the wooden frames to prepare for a fresh coat.

> **ROSE:** *First, with a putty knife, I removed the dried, broken putty and replaced it with fresh, soft putty. The next day, after the putty dried, I painted the frame a beautiful dark green Mom had chosen. We painted the frames because it was less expensive than buying shutters.*

The garage was also where we kept our one bicycle — the one the three older girls used when they were old enough to ride. That old blue bike gave many hours of delight.

> **CAROL:** *I don't remember ever riding this bicycle to country school although many kids rode their bikes to school. What I remember is going out on Highway 65 in front of our house for an afternoon spin. I'd peddle up the half-mile incline, which took lots of effort. But the breeze flowing through my hair as I coasted downhill was a treat.*

Dad did not want Rose to ride the bus to high school. Three neighbor boys were driving to school each day, so it was arranged for Rose to travel to school with them in their large green Buick during her sophomore and junior years of high school. They graduated a year before she did. This mode of transportation was more economical and took care of the bus situation.

The boys had graduated when Rose was a high school senior. She was allowed — even encouraged — to drive to school using that old Dodge pick-up. Our parents were practical. They knew if we drove our own car to school, we'd be home at least thirty minutes before the bus would have gotten us there, giving us more time to help with chores and field work. The school bus ride would have taken one hour each way.

Years later, Dad told us another reason he preferred we

drive the family vehicle to high school. He knew we would hear, see, and learn things on the school bus that were not appropriate for his teenage daughters. He trusted our driving ability and we did not abuse his trust.

ROSE: *With a driver's license and permission to drive, a group of high school girlfriends would gather on Friday night to tour the town. We'd all pile into one sedan and drive around looking for other friends doing the same. Favorite stops were the roller-skating rink, drive-in movie theatre, and the drive-in A&W Root Beer stand. At the end of the evening, we each gave a quarter to the driver, who filled the car with one dollar's worth of gas. The car arrived home with a full tank.*

I drove the pick-up to high school my senior year and wanted so badly to be in the high school play. However, Dad needed me at home to work on the farm and would not spare me for after-school hours of play practice.

Rose

Dad purchased a 1955 car—a brand-new Dodge sedan—black and white with tail wings—a sleek-looking dash of beauty. We had the money to do this partly because Dad stopped drinking in 1954. Less time and money spent at the liquor store meant money left for the family. What a change from the small stick-shift pick-up to a car with power steering and turn signals. Imagine not having to stick an arm out the window to hand-signal a stop, right or left turn.

Carol

CAROL: *Returning from a visit with Dad's cousin, Dad and Mom decided that I could drive while they took the back seat. I tooled along without a care, listening to the folks talk, until I noticed something in the rear-view mirror: a car with a flashing red light on its roof! Minutes later, a policeman was telling me that he was going eighty miles an hour and I was gaining on him. I was dumbfounded. I hadn't realized that car had so much power. I sure wish I'd had cruise control then. I had to travel alone to the next county to pay for the ticket out of my own money. Twenty-five dollars! That was a big chunk of the money I had earned working in the school cafeteria.*

Maybe the money did not come for working in the school cafeteria. It could have come from other long hours of labor. We were expected to contribute to the family by helping with chores and field work. We did not receive an allowance, but on occasion we were given small wages. Dad paid me forty cents an hour for working in the fields. Sitting at the wheel, cultivating up and down long rows of corn for hours, was monotonous. It was also a challenge to stay awake. Often, I sang or

47

*prayed the Rosary—pressing a different finger on the
wheel until I reached ten—the number of Hail Mary's
in each decade. Praying while doing a repetitive job
was something I'd learned while gardening with Mom.
As we picked beans or peas, which could be tedious,
we prayed the Rosary out loud together.*

Years later, Rose worked as a 4-H extension agent in the
neighboring county and lived at home. Even though she'd
been driving for many years, she made a costly mistake as
she drove away from the farm.

ROSE: *As I drove away that beautiful morning, I
noted a funny rattling sound. I thought, "Hmm, this
sounds like the car on a cold winter morning when it
just needs to warm up." But it wasn't a cold morning
at all. I continued driving, listening to the noise as the
car slowed. Yes, it stopped dead in its tracks. I had just
burned out the engine! Not a pleasant scene for Dad
or me. Dad had neglected to replace the plug in the oil
drain pan the evening before when he changed the oil
and I was not bright enough to recognize the warning
sign.*

THE GRANARY

A granary is a building used to store grains, a generic term that includes wheat, oats, barley, rye, millet, shelled or ground corn, rice, and even popcorn. A two-story granary on the Deml farm stored wheat loosely in the dry area upstairs. In the center of the building, an open area beneath a drop-down stairway contained gunny sacks filled with ground feed for chickens and the pails used to carry feed to the chickens or pigs.

Pails of feed were carried from the granary to the hen house past the added granary extension. This extension was made of corrugated tin. The tin was used on the walls and siding to make a shed for the tractor. Walking to the hen house, Carol trailed the fingers of her left hand along the siding, making her fingers jump like a truck jerking down a bumpy gravel road. She carried either grain from the granary or water from the milk house to the hens in the chicken house.

Carol, Cathy and Rose

The chickens milled around her legs in happy greeting. She emptied the five-gallon pail of feed by pouring it into the round hanging feeders. Only a bit of grain or nutritious chicken feed seeped out into the bottom, like excess water escaping a flower planter. Because chickens naturally peck for their food, scattered feed resulted, but these containers prevented much waste.

Carol carried water into the building and emptied the fountains of straw and other debris before filling them with fresh water.

Returning to the granary, on one side of the drop-down stairway on the ground floor was a bin for grain. On the other side, a storage area held loose ground corn. The stairway, really an open-backed ladder on the first floor, was usually hinged up to the ceiling on a hook. This ladder could be lowered only with caution. When not in use, it remained raised.

After harvest, grain was elevator-transferred from a truck to the second floor of the granary and it flowed into a large heap in the middle of the upstairs room. Later, we shoveled enough grain to last several weeks through a hole in the floor to the ground level. When more grain was needed, Dad lowered the ladder and we went up into the storage area to shovel grain into the lower bin.

> **CAROL:** *The ladder was heavy. As a teenager, I sometimes needed to lower it in order to go up and push grain to the bin below. On one occasion as I began to lower the ladder, I was caught off-balance, fell forward and my nose banged onto a rung of the heavy ladder as the ladder clunked to the floor. That stung. No blood drained from my nose, but tears spilled from my eyes as the pain punctured my brain cells to alert them of the accident.*
>
> *The doctor's verdict? "The break will leave your nose flattened a bit, but there has been no serious injury to the workings inside."*

Unusual events can happen anywhere on a farm. Carol found that out the hard way.

CAROL: *A stray dog stood in the granary doorway. He acted as though he owned the place. With my hand extended, I talked gently to the beast as I walked forward to get at the grain needed to complete my chores. I approached reluctantly and cautiously. Because I loved our dogs and had never experienced anything but friendly licks and attention from them, I was surprised when the animal growled. As I grew closer to the steps, he jumped forward and grabbed my fingers between his strong teeth. Skin broke. Off I ran to the house in tears to report my terror.*

This time the doctor's response was, "You need a tetanus shot to prevent infection that could cause lockjaw—muscle spasms developing in the jaw and elsewhere in the body."

Lockjaw did not develop, thank goodness, and the incident gave me a healthy wariness of strange animals.

Dad discovered the dog belonged to our next-door neighbor who usually tied it securely. Because the animal had shown viciousness in our yard, our good friend shot his well-loved animal-turned-ogre.

Summertime harvest and daily chores carrying feed from the granary to pigs and chickens around the farmyard remind us of the granary.

PIG HOUSES

The pigs on our farm had a variety of places for shelter: sometimes indoors; sometimes outdoors.

Close to the house between the corncrib and house stood a long low shack with a series of pens to hold piglets. A simple black tar-paper roof covered this flat low building, a perfect height for climbing. We girls climbed onto that rickety roof of the pig house...a scary trek, but adventurous; we wondered if we would fall through the holes. We survived the daring act.

> **ROSE:** *A small back yard was neatly mowed near this pig pen. If we three girls were not in the house playing paper dolls (cutting out and dressing them from pictures in the Sears catalog), we played dolls or house outdoors.*
>
> *Gathering soft fresh cut grass clippings, we climbed to the top of the shack to play house. Using the grass clippings to lay out rooms for our paper dolls, we became interior designers and architects of our dream homes. Acorns, corn kernels, and dandelions colorfully decorated our lovely designs.*

Another building, a low ramshackle one, hidden in a grove to the west of the granary—far from the house—sheltered the pigs. Yes, pigs smell, although they are considered "clean" animals. Many farmers said, "Pigs smell like money," meaning pigs offer farmers a short cash crop.

From the back door of the milk house, twice daily at approximately 6:30 a.m. and 4:00 p.m., as well as on weekends and holidays, we lugged two five-gallon buckets of water out to the pigs. The splashing water from the buckets on our legs felt good in the summer time, but in the winter it led to frozen jeans clinging to our legs.

Grain and slop (a mixture of ground corn and water, but any other vegetable remains and sour milk might be added) were carried to the pigs. We poured the pigs' feed into a long low trough where the pigs lined up side-by-side to eat. Noisy sows grunted and greedily shoved to be first in line for dried, dented corn-on-the-cob, which was thrown in the center of the floor, or the slop poured into the trough.

ROSE: *Now, I like pigs, but fierce rats lined up along the trough with the pigs. Although I was afraid of the rats, I carried the slop and poured it into the feeder. I hated those varmints with a passion. There were so many fearsome rats lined up to eat that Dad took a shotgun and with one shot down the line was able to kill several at a time.*

At last the building was bulldozed and the rats no longer had a hiding place nor an easy source of food. Our small dog, a rat terrier, would search out the rat holes, dig into the tunnel and grab the rat and snap its neck. Our dog definitely discouraged the rats from relocating to another area of the yard.

We had to clean the pig sty on a regular basis. Pigs, like cows, are susceptible to hoof rot if allowed to wander through their own excrement for any length of time. We shoveled two portions of the long building's cement floors.

Another extension of the pig house had no cement floor but a straw-laden room where the pigs slept in the wintertime. We used a pitch fork to remove old soiled straw from that dirt floor.

After Dad sold all of the Herefords, he destroyed the ramshackle shed and used the barn to raise hogs. With better lighting and ventilation, each sow had her own stall—built on the cement floor with wooden boards closely enclosing her body. The stall prevented the sow from rolling over and crushing a piglet. The lowest boards were high enough for the cute little piglets to run freely beneath them, scamper away and avoid accidental squashing by the mama pig.

Dad would say, "Pick up one of those piglets; hold it; rub it against your cheek. The hair on the warm piglet's body is soft."

Sows are mature female pigs; boars are mature males. The term pigs is generic for any age or gender. Sows delivered as many as sixteen piglets. They suckled at the sow's teats, like a milk machine attached to two rows of buttons down the underbelly of their mother. When sufficiently nurtured, they were weaned and fed twice daily—fresh food and fresh water. Pigs never lived for a long period of time on our farm because Dad raised them to sell for profit after they grew to the exact market size.

According to 21st century standards, today's pig barns hold an average of 3,000 pigs, provide technological tools to measure and deliver nutrient-laden corn supplies, and water spigots—so there is no need to carry food and water.

The pigs raised on our farm spent many hours outside the building. Pigs roll in mud to keep cool. Confined to a building, the pigs of today don't get to play in the mud.

One summer Dad moved the pigs across the gravel road to a fenced-in grove closer to the fields. Old trees had been removed to make more tillable land for crops and some had been cut for fire wood. The grove was slowly made smaller and smaller.

Dad had planted fast-growing evergreens to form a windbreak between the grove and the garden, to protect the buildings from the strong winter winds, and to provide additional borders as a backdrop for our massive gardens and the house. These two, full-grown, beautiful rows of evergreens separated the pigs from the buildings.

> **CAROL:** *I remember the day Dad lost his wallet. He reached into his back pocket and discovered it was missing. All of us looked for the treasure which housed his cash, social security card and driver's license—no credit cards were used then—but to no avail. Much fussing occurred; Dad obtained a new driver's license and social security card and then the inner turmoil finally ceased.*
>
> *The next spring when he was out mowing around the blue spruce trees near the summer pigpen, he discovered his wallet. Much jubilation ensued over this rescue just because he knew its whereabouts. No one had stolen it. No pigs had gotten into it.*

Each year we butchered a pig for our own use. After its throat was slit, the pig was hung by its back legs with head down and its throat draining blood. Dad took the butchered pig to the Owatonna locker plant. At the locker, chops, ribs, and roasts were cut, packaged, frozen, and stored in our numbered unit.

Before the purchase of a home freezer, we drove into Owatonna once a week to get our own meat and keep it for the week in a small freezer within the refrigerator. The rented locker, similar to locked boxes at a bus depot that store luggage until departure time, contained all the meat from a butchered pig and the meat from a beef side.

Every part of the pig was used. This explains the saying, "All but the pig's squeal." Other delicacies made at home included head cheese and kroupe (pronounced crow-pea), a Bohemian breakfast treat, a mixture of barley, ground pork organs and spices.

CAROL: *Uncle Henry and Rose both remember kroupe. Uncle Henry described the process of preparing this food, "They made kroupe out of the tongue, the brain, barley and head blood. And it was good, too. And then they would take the intestines from a hog and wash them out real good. We pumped a handle on one end of a little machine until the mixture flowed through the machine into an intestine and became a sausage."*

There are many recipes for ethnic foods as well as many ways to store and preserve the food.

ROSE: *We stored our kroupe in a big gallon crock and we'd scoop out whatever we wanted for breakfast. This is an example of an economical, fast food of the day, but it was certainly no favorite of mine. The unappetizing kroupe looked like tiny greasy black and white peas.*

CORNCRIBS

Dad tore down and hauled away the falling-down shack of a pig house that was used for baby pigs. Next to the single corncrib, Dad built another corncrib, a double one, in place of the pig house. In this large building, he made sure there was enough space for farm implement storage between a crib on either side beneath its peaked roof. Looking at old photos, we see lots of friends came for a big celebration following completion of that construction.

A single corncrib that stored dried corn-on-the-cob to feed the hogs stood across from the chicken house. It was a peek-a-boo building made of boards. An inch or two of space between each board allowed air to travel inside to dry the corn. When we removed a bushel of corn, a bunch of the cobs from further up the crib would slide down, like children sliding down a curly slide. From the narrow slatted corncrib, we carried several arm loads of dry ear corn to a hand sheller in the granary. The corn was shelled for the chickens and we threw the cobs to the pigs.

From the gleanings of the corn sheller, we used the now-empty corn cobs and the dropped bits of shelled corn to create the toys and games of the day.

CAROL: *Cathy and I made mud pies near the corncrib. Once the crib was emptied and waiting for* *the next year's crop, we could store our dried mud artistry in the crib. The intensity of making these mud pies proved helpful for Cathy when she served culinary tidbits to guests in her later years. I myself make a mean pie—apple, rhubarb, cherry, green tomato mincemeat, pecan, and strawberry.*

Thanks to Rose's 4-H pie crust demonstration, for which she won a trip to the Minnesota State Fair, I absorbed her zillion practice efforts that resulted in flaky and tender crusts for all my pies.

Because baking seemed to be a chore for Mom, Rose decided to learn to bake in order to help her and relieve her of that unnecessary stress.

ROSE: *Pie crust has only four ingredients—flour, lard, salt and water. I attempted to make this one evening when the folks were visiting the neighbors. Out came the recipe, ingredients and directions. I must have done something right because I soon had a dough ball.*

It looked totally unappetizing—like a sticky, gray lump of clay. I threw it out for the dog to eat. Guilt stalked me because we never wasted anything. Well, even the dog sniffed it in disapproval.

This first attempt did not discourage Rose, and with much persistence she learned to make great pie crust and demonstrated this at the Minnesota State Fair where she won a blue ribbon and several pieces of baking equipment. Demonstrations were meant to teach the public and also teach the 4-H member skills in public speaking.

FIELD WORK

Dad enlarged the granary for storage of equipment. He sold the horses and purchased a tractor. Dad soon acquired larger pieces of farm equipment. The four-row corn planter, a wire baler, and a wheat combine required the construction of an open tin machine shed attached to the west of the granary. He built another corrugated tin shed to the north of the granary to house the tractor. There is now a corridor of buildings—the granary, attached tractor shed and chicken house that border the lane to the field.

We inspected the machinery in preparation for field work. In mid-March the snows began to melt and Dad brought the grain seeder out of storage for inspection and greasing.

ROSE: *It was my job to dry-brush any rust on the movable parts of the machine. Dad would bring the heavy grease gun and point out all spots that needed grease. Not only was this tool long and bulky to manipulate, it required much strength to aim and connect the tip of the gun to the joint and then squeeze out the rather solid grease into the appropriate opening. I learned the location of grease spots of all the machines. Interesting that I could do this then, but in later years I no longer have any mechanical abilities.*

We used the grain seeder to plant the first crop which was a mixture of alfalfa and grain seeds which could withstand a late spring frost. Corn was planted much later because it could not tolerate unexpected frosts. The young corn shoots were easily damaged by even a light frost. Using a carpenter's pencil, Dad carefully recorded planting and harvest dates on a beam in the granary. What a quick reference—a farmer's personal almanac.

The grain seeder was one of the oldest pieces of equipment on the farm and was put into winter storage in a lean-to attached to the rear of the granary. Our old team of horses, Tom and Jerry, pulled this machine many years. Dad converted this hook-up to be pulled by the tractor.

The seeder completed three tasks at once: it dug rows in the dirt, dropped seed through long tubes into the row, and dragged a series of rings behind each tube to cover the seed. When all parts operated correctly, the tubes distributed the very tiny alfalfa seeds.

Two crops were planted at once with the grain seeder. The oats came up quickly and were harvested in early August. Alfalfa sprouted and grew slowly and remained a short plant. The grain was cut above it and alfalfa survived the winter. The alfalfa was cut for hay the following year. If lucky, with an exceptional growing season, three cuttings of hay might be harvested in one summer.

The horse-drawn seeder was designed to be observed by the driver who was riding on the rear of the machine behind the boxes of seeds and tubes. Alfalfa seeds were expensive and needed to be spread very evenly to insure a heavy yield the following season. The driver would check that the tubes allowed a steady flow of seeds. A long square rod or shaft below the seed boxes turned with the machine wheels to activate the seed-dropping.

Our old team of horses, Tom and Jerry, no longer on our farm, had pulled the seeder many years. After the purchase of a tractor, the driver is now on the tractor—not behind the seed boxes. Dad assigned someone to ride on the seeder to check the flow of seeds.

Converted grain seeder and tractor

ROSE: *Dad, driving the new tractor and pulling the converted seeder, assigned me to ride along to check the flow of the seeds. What a joy to ride along behind the boxes on a beautiful spring day. However, driving into the bright sunlight, I could not see the tiny seeds but knew that I must keep checking the flow. I stretched forward my left, gloved hand to catch the falling seed. My oversized soft gloves were quickly caught by the revolving square shaft and drew my fingers and hand around and into the machine.*

I screamed and Dad immediately stopped. No blood in sight, no immediate pain to indicate broken bones. Dad now faced the problem of how to remove my hand, which was tightly wrapped around the shaft.

Dad decided the only thing he could do to release my hand was unhook the tractor, drive home, get a handsaw, lower the cut drive-shaft and slide my hand from the rod.

The accident occurred one-half mile from the farmstead at the far end of our farm. For this emergency, the tools Dad needed were in the garage. Before the days of cell phones, the only phone was in the house.

Dad drove away on the tractor and I remained joined to the shaft with my hand wrapped tightly around it. Our wonderful, faithful, watchful, farm dog, Teddy, sat with me waiting for Dad's return. Feeling quite trapped, I have since wondered if this increased the feelings of claustrophobia that I now have.

It seemed hours later that Dad returned, driving the pick-up and carrying a saw and other tools he thought might be necessary to free my hand. The shaft had to be released from the wheels. He sawed and separated the rod, lowered it to an angle, and carefully slid my gloved hand off the rod.

Still holding my gloved hand, stiffened from the clawed position, I was seated in the middle of the truck with Mom and Dad to drive into town to see the doctor. We were all afraid to take off the glove for fear that a very numb finger or fingers would come off inside the glove.

The doctor gently felt my hand, cut off the glove and slowly extended one, two, three, four fingers. No cuts, no breaks, but one very swollen ring finger. There was a great sigh of relief from all in the room when the doctor cut off THE RING and sent me home with fingers intact, although a bit stiff and curved.

Rose soon had other chores and work to do in the fields and Carol began to ride on the seeder.

CAROL: *One spring day Dad asked me to watch the seeder as he planted wheat. I was happy to do this task. As we seeded, an idea struck me.*

"Dad, Dad." I called.

He stopped the tractor and came around to investigate the problem. Because he saw no problem, he looked at me quizzically.

I said, "April Fool's."

I think it was the only time I caught him on an April Fool's Day over the years. I was delighted to catch him after all the times he tricked me.

When fall arrives, mature grain fields become heavy with seeds and turn a beautiful golden color. If a heavy rain and wind storm arrives near harvest time, it will twist and lodge the grain in such a way that the machines can not cut the grain nor lift and tie it into bundles. At harvest time, a grain binder cut swaths of grain and automatically tied the bundles that it deposited on the field. Men followed behind, gathered six or eight bundles, and shaped them into mini-straw stacks, called shocks. The shocks were scattered haphazardly around the field. This was a method of holding the grain upright in the fields waiting, possibly several days for the arrival of the threshing machine. The yield could be anticipated by noting the number of grain shocks in the field.

A grain thresher is a monster machine that was moved from farm to farm. The machine was placed near the barn and readied for threshing. Crews of six or more men drove into the fields with their large hayracks. Moving slowly past the shocks of grain, the men used a three-tined bundle fork to lift and toss the bundles from each shock onto the rack. The racks were filled as high as possible to avoid unnecessary, time-consuming trips from the fields to the threshing machine.

The light-weight three-tined bundle fork is still used in gardens. This fork was also used to harvest potatoes grown in lightweight, loose, sandy soil.

Horses or tractors pulled the racks adjacent to the thresher and the men again threw the bundles into the thresher which devoured the bundles and separated kernels of grain from the straw. The grain was funneled into wagons and the awkward gooseneck-like arm, called a stacker, blew the straw into piles, near the barn. The grain was hauled to an elevator that carried it up into the granary.

After the conversion to combining wheat, Carol recalls the golden sunshine rippling over the fresh and musty-smelling wheat as it dusted up the elevator into the sturdy granary. With her bare feet spread apart on top of the grain in the truck bed, she shoveled the pearly pieces from the truck into the elevator. This annual summer task took place so the chickens would have their feed throughout the winter months. The elevator extended to the top of the granary where the grain spewed—through an uncovered square hole—into a heap on the upper level of the building.

Neighbors gathered to help each other during grain harvest and haying season. The farmers rested, visited, and ate together. Hearty lunches were served in the morning and afternoon. Some of Rose's favorite picnic recipes of bars, sandwiches, prune biscuits, and lemonade still remind her of those lunches.

Dream Bars:

Combine with a blender to the size of oatmeal: 1 C. flour, ½ C. brown sugar and ½ C. butter. Press into a 9" x 9" pan. Bake in a 350° oven for 15-20 minutes.

Whisk together: 2 eggs and 1 C. brown sugar.

Mix dry ingredients: 2 T. flour, 2 tsp. baking powder and ¼ tsp. salt.

Blend dry ingredients with egg mixture.

Stir in: 1 tsp. vanilla, 1 C. coconut and ½ C. chopped walnuts. Pour over the baked layer.

Bake for 20 minutes in 350° oven. Makes 25 squares.

Meanwhile, the women prepared food all day long. Harvest might take three days on one farm. A minimum of ten men were fed at a 10 a.m. lunch, a noon dinner, and a 3 p.m. lunch. The men had to return home to do evening chores so a supper meal was not served unless rain threatened to destroy the remaining harvest. In that case, men worked until dark which required the women folk at home to do the evening chores.

The morning and afternoon lunches consisted of sandwiches, cookies, bars and/or cake, and lemonade to quench thirst. Gallons of coffee were served throughout the day. An egg was added to the coffee grounds and poured directly into boiling water. This egg coffee was usually made in a two-gallon enamel coffee pot. The egg acted as a clarifier and also helped settle the grounds to the bottom of the pot. Not all women mastered the art of making clear, delicious coffee. Some farms had very poor or sulfurous water that tasted nasty no matter what they tried.

These were days that girls helped in the kitchen and were not in the fields. Although many farm women worked and spent hours in the fields, Mom did not drive tractor or work in our fields, but we daughters helped in the fields.

The farmer watches the crops change as the months pass. The grain, alfalfa and corn have been planted. The corn is cultivated. The hay is cut, raked, baled and stored in the barn. Just as late frost threatened the corn crop, the farmer again watches the threatening rain clouds. If the hay has been cut and a heavy rain occurs, the hay may lie in the fields so long that it rots and cannot be harvested. At other times of lighter rainfall, many of the nutrients are leached out of the hay. Farming is a gamble.

Haying season was the best time of the year. Rose loved to rake hay, see the clouds in the sky, and smell the fragrance of fresh cut alfalfa and clover. Hay must be cut during a dry spell between frequent spring rains. It needs to lie in the field about three days to dry enough to be turned and rolled into narrow rows for the baling machine to pick, bale, and drop in the field.

Other things happened in the open hayfields after harvest. Learning to drive was a major growing-up experience. Most farm children learn to drive while quite young, first with tractors and then with farm vehicles in the open field. Not much chance of an accident, you are thinking.

ROSE: *One sunny day, Dad was baling hay. I was in the field with the pick-up. It held supplies that might be needed: extra gas, small tools and extra wire for the baler. Also, important to Dad, we always carried sandwiches, cookies or bars, candy, water and beer.*

Sitting in the truck, I noticed Dad signaling from the far end of the field to drive over with the supplies. Quickly, I started the pick-up, shifted the gears, let out the clutch and began to drive across the field dotted with bales of hay. I turned the pick-up towards the corner of the field where Dad waited. As I turned the truck, I could not see one bale in front of the right wheel. The wire-tied hay bales, about four feet long and two feet square, weigh approximately eighty-five pounds and are dropped from the bailer randomly around the field.

"Get moving," Dad called.

Not so fast. As I stepped on the gas, the pick-up tried to move, up and over the bale that would not budge. Instead the right fender on the pick-up obligingly lifted and bent outwards right up and over that bale. Scrape! Grate! Rasp! Crunch!

I stopped the car and jumped out to check the damage. I could see Dad striding across the field towards the truck to see WHY I had stopped.

Dad paused, looked over the situation, checked for damage and said, "Well. No one is hurt, nothing seems to be broken. I'll just remove the bale and bend that fender back into shape."

In truth, a field is a great place for driver's education, the formal version of which took place in town for Rose several years later. Two things were emphasized in driver's education class. The first involved hand signals. The driver rolled down the window and extended his left arm to signal. A raised-up arm indicated a right turn. An arm extended straight out was a signal to turn left. If the arm dangled next to the door, it signaled that the car was slowing down. The second instruction stressed the need to look carefully both ways at an intersection and when backing up the car. Rose lost points in one driver's exam when she did not turn her head both right and left to check if a car might be in her path.

ROSE: *A frightening car experience occurred before I had a driver's license. Mom and I drove away from Kelly's Department Store heading for home. Mom did not drive often and she panicked in this situation. As she started across the highway to make a left-hand turn, she released the clutch too quickly and the car jerked.*

Thinking it was an engine problem, she reached for the choke on the dashboard. By mistake she pulled the throttle which is like stepping on the gas. The pick-up accelerated. We rapidly speeded ahead as the left-hand turn took us across the highway and into the gas station where the truck was still turning left through the pumps.

Mom was gripping the steering wheel, not knowing what to do next. Luckily, I had driven the truck in the fields and I recognized the problem. I reached across the dashboard, pushed in the throttle to stop the excess flow of gas and turned the key that switched off the ignition.

The pick-up slowed to a stop. Mom composed herself and we drove home, thankful that our guardian angels had made sure there was no traffic in our way.

Farms abutted each other in 80- or 160-acre plots. Our farm was one-half mile deep to the west and one-quarter mile wide bordering the busy north-south paved highway. This was US Highway 65, paved all the way to New Orleans and heavily traveled in front of our land.

Farmers wanted to plant corn as early as possible and still avoid heavy spring rains that could make field work impossible. If corn was planted too early, the early sprouts could be killed by a late frost. Nature provided a reliable clue for us, however. Oak trees are the last to bud out and farmers watched and waited for the budding. When the oak trees budded out, it was safe to plant corn and, hopefully this was before the first of June because everyone watched for the corn to be knee high by the fourth of July.

Hybrid seed corn companies gave Dad a discounted price for seed corn that would be seen as an advertisement for that company. Corn identification signs were placed at the end of each row so they could be seen by all passing vehicles. Dad planted this identified seed corn in beautiful rows perpendicular to the highway. He prided himself on his ability to plant the straightest rows in the county. And the seed companies competed to get his business to advertise and show off the newest corn available.

Corn was planted by machine. Three kernels were placed in each hill. Three plants, spaced apart in a hill, allowed sunlight to reach every plant from all sides. Twenty-four inches between the rows and hills in each row allowed for cross cultivation. We could cultivate up the rows and across the rows. Cultivating removes weeds, loosens and aerates the soil, while mounding it close to the plant to add stability to the stalk that eventually yields long, heavy ears of corn. A weed-free field will yield a heavy production and clean crop.

Every young farm child of that era dreaded the day or days when everyone went into the corn field to chop out or hoe thistles to remove that noxious weed. The roots of thistles grew deep and the cultivator scooted around the roots rather than removed them, making it necessary to weed thistles manually.

The corn was planted in hills of three to provide support for each stalk to hold the heavy ears that would soon develop. Corn has shallow roots and the close planting in hills also provided some protection from the winds and heavy rains that might blow them down.

Today corn is not planted in hills but rather close to each other—every few inches. Cultivation was less necessary when farmers began to use more chemical weed killers. Even that is changing with the business of agriculture and differs from region to region because of soil and water and weather conditions. For example, in Idaho the rainfall is much different than in southern Minnesota and farmers grow wonderful corn using irrigation. Corn has been hybridized to produce many more ears per stalk and the height of a corn plant has even been modified to suit the purpose and produce a yield of more and more bushels of corn per acre.

> **ROSE:** *I enjoyed hours of quiet time driving the tractor with the attached corn cultivator in June. The rows were straight, weed free—in a word, picture perfect. That is, until I fell asleep driving the tractor while cultivating corn. On this lovely spring day with soft, soothing, warm sunshine and fluffy white clouds, it was just me and my tractor drifting near the highway. My daydreaming almost became a nightmare. I dozed while the tractor kept slowly moving, gently removing about thirty feet of corn in this row. Yes, this was the end of the row in plain view of all cars driving past.*
>
> *I jumped off the tractor, ran back, replanted each corn plant, but to no avail. That was in 1953, with a two-row cultivator, so no extreme damage occurred. The damage today would be extensive with a twelve-row cultivator. Also, farms have grown from 160 acres to 1600 acres. Be alert. Corn does not like to be transplanted. I never again slept at the wheel.*

If it's raining, go fishing. A mini-fishing vacation could happen on a rainy day. Mother accompanied Dad on fishing trips, sometimes rising at three or four a.m. to fish on a northern Minnesota lake.

Dad would say, "It's raining, Elsie. We can't be in the

fields for the next few days. Let's go fishing." A note on the table gave Rose instructions to do the outdoor chores, cooking and baking, and watch Cathy and Carol until their return.

A good fisherwoman, seated quietly in the boat and wearing a warm jacket to keep out the early morning chill, Mother pulled in fish—sometimes hauling in the only catch of the day, much to Dad's chagrin.

Dad and Mon

Dad always enjoyed fishing during a lull in the growing season. Although we lived near Turtle Creek, it was not a good source for fish. Bullheads growing in the cold Minnesota rivers were tasty. Fishing for walleye, pike, or bullheads was the one Minnesota sport we could not do on our farm. It required a short drive to the river.

> **ROSE:** *Fish were easily caught with a cane pole and angle worm. Dad took me early one spring morning an hour away to a great fishing hole under a bridge. We quickly caught our limit, picked up the pail filled with fish, and started to climb up to the road. We looked up to see the game and fish warden standing there.*
>
> *He asked, "Do you not know that fishing season begins next week?" Red-faced, we returned the fish to the river and drove home empty-handed. This was definitely a fish story to remember.*

70

LAWNS AND GARDENS

Mom enjoyed the mini-fishing vacations but spent many more hours at home tending her lawns, flower and vegetable gardens.

Strawberry beds edged the cornfield beyond the summertime wooded pig yard. We picked pans and pans and pans of strawberries. On our knees, bending over the strawberry patch—not in rows, we played hide-and-seek with the leaves to search for the prize. Oftentimes, we popped the tasty morsels into our mouths. We were busy both picking and eating.

Mom, Eileen, Rose, Leona, Irene

Mom made strawberry jam. Mom canned strawberries. Before the purchase of a home freezer, we froze many dozens of quart bags of berries and took them to our locker in Owatonna. After we got a freezer, we continued freezing strawberries for our eating pleasure during the winter months. We ate strawberries for breakfast, lunch, dinner and in-between. Fresh strawberries on freshly-baked bread topped with our cow's rich cream treated us with a special welcome after school. We never sold strawberries because most farms had gardens and their own strawberry patches.

Dad's favorite berry was the raspberry. Thus, the raspberry patch was expanded more than once. We stood picking them with long-sleeved shirts covering our arms for protection from both mosquito bites and thorny raspberry stalks. Mom had a natural resistance to mosquito bites, but she covered her arms to prevent scratches from thorns. The crop of juicy berries yielded less than the strawberries, but the taste was heavenly.

Her gardens went beyond those wonderful patches of strawberries and raspberries. She could be found picking green beans, peas, onions, ground-cherries, rhubarb, tomatoes, cucumbers, and other foods that were used for meals in the summer. These foods also were preserved for winter use.

Mom loved the out-of-doors. Beyond the outhouse and the house, the front lawn spread up to and beyond the clotheslines. Dad planted blue spruce evergreens in clumps of three in several locations on the lawn. Mom grew flower beds as an edging that separated the green lawn from the vegetable garden.

The flowers—gladioli and more gladioli, lilac bushes, petunias and zinnias, impatiens, tulips and daffodils— formed a border between the lawn and the garden.

Anyone who drove into the yard could see our attractive white two-story home. The house faced the highway. Its big front porch was screened, and its corners were hung with clematis vines that flowered beautifully each spring. Around the foundation were a number of nicely trimmed and shaped white spirea bushes.

CAROL: *Once Cathy was enticed to one of the bushes by a drone of buzzing. The buzzing was coming from bees searching for nectar. Cathy started plucking the bees off the shrubbery one by one and crushing them between her fingers. That is, until one of them stung her. Tears rolled down her face and that game ended fast.*

At the side of the house were two fragrant flowering shrubs: a mock orange and a lilac. They separated the lawn from our large flower and vegetable garden. A row of iris grew alongside the hedge. Behind them, Mom always planted a row of gladioli for summer cutting.

Mom was attracted to beautiful flower gardens, and new plants fascinated her. She asked relatives, neighbors or friends for a clipping of something that caught her eye in their gardens. Knowing she had a green thumb, friends responded to her curiosity and were eager to share seedlings, clippings, and bulbs with her.

Mom loved flowers. In the summertime, when the gladioli, favorites of ours, were in full bloom, she cut dozens of them and other summer flowers. She placed them on the large oak dining room table in the kitchen. But before the flowers ended up on the table, Mom would store them in the basement.

CAROL: *As a child, I always wondered why Mom put the flowers in the basement. After all, no one went to the basement just to see glads.*

It was cooler down there, so they lasted longer. A cool, dark spot slowed the opening of florets and extended the life of the flowers. And then Mom could choose the best time to show them off upstairs.

Mom also loved to share her flowers with others. Visitors to our house, even unexpected ones, might be surprised with the gift of a beautiful bouquet. The lilac bush gave us ample lilacs to share. Mom often sent us girls to Sister School with a bouquet of lilacs and spirea for the nuns. If the growing season cooperated, we could also take peonies or lily-of-the-valley blooms to school.

The lawn grew wider as Mom cleared brush from land surrounding our buildings. Sometimes she got up at dawn on hot summer days to mow with the push mower. Other times we kids mowed—in the apple orchard all the way from the barn's east fence to the highway, behind the chicken house, around the blue spruce trees near the summertime pig yard, between all the buildings, behind and in front of the house all the way to the highway. She repeatedly cleared more spaces to create a wide-open look at our farm from the highway. People often commented about the lovely sight.

Soon the lawn spread into the groves behind the chicken house close to the grove where the pigs loved to cool off in the mud.

An ugly, rickety, old barbed-wire fence divided a pasture by the barn from the orchard lawn. Eventually, when animals were no longer pastured inside it, Mom and Carol tore the fence down. The good part of that was that Dad replaced it with a wooden one that matched the fence between the milk house and the garage. Painted white, this new fence spiffed up our property's appearance.

The not-so-good part was that Mom and Carol found partially-to-empty whiskey bottles planted beside some of the posts, evidence of Dad's drinking, which steadily grew worse.

Rose

74

When not assigned the task of mowing the lawn, we found many ways to enjoy our beautiful areas of lawn. We even had names for the three areas: back lawn, front lawn, and the orchard lawn (not creative names but each area had a purpose). The front lawn gradually sloped down to the highway. This ten-foot slope or decline was the perfect place for rolling downhill but not steep enough for us to gather speed. Our slow, gentle rolls ended just at the edge of the gravel shoulder on the edge of the highway.

Meanwhile, people enjoyed viewing the lawns and gardens as they zoomed down the highway. They were surprised by falling apples on the orchard side of our driveway.

ROSE: *The "Greening" apple tree, an old heritage tree in the corner of the orchard near our driveway and the highway, had low, sturdy, spreading branches, perfect for climbing and sitting. Up in the tree, hidden in the cool leaves, we enjoyed watching the cars and trucks drive by. We threw small green apples onto the road to see if they would be crushed by the cars. The apples usually missed their mark and simply bounced along the road—BUT—not always. If an apple hit the car or was seen falling onto the road, the driver would slow down and look around and around. We quickly disappeared and let the driver think the wind had caused the apples to fall.*

Some cars and trucks disregarded the 55 miles-an-hour speed limit. Because the lawn was on a hill high enough for us to see the passengers in cars, we sometimes sat waving at passing motorists. Most friendly semi-truck drivers waved; some pulled the cord to honk the horn at us.

CAROL: *Dropping apples onto the highway must have given Cathy the idea to throw stones at passing cars. Not such a good idea because a stone struck and* *cracked the windshield of a passing car. The driver turned around, pulled into the circle drive and waited for Dad's approach. Called to the scene by Dad, Cathy and I listened to the man speak. After the driver explained the situation, Dad paid for the window. This was a prickly and worrisome time for us as we waited and listened. Without further comment, Dad left. I think he felt we'd had our punishment.*

Mom's idea of appearance extended to the first impressions people would have as they drove by or entered our driveway. This required hours of work to maintain the park-like appearance. Each of us was expected to help with yard work. We spent many hours raking and mowing—long before yard care became a business. No one hired lawn care service. We mowed and trimmed the front lawn, the back lawn, and the orchard lawn. These areas of lawn kept us occupied pushing the lawnmower. Yes, there is such a thing as a rotary push mower.

Our house was located on a slight incline above the chicken house and corncribs. This area of lawn seemed like a hill when we were mowing it. Hilly is a relative term in the eyes of a small child. In reality, southern Minnesota is flat as a pancake.

The lawns provided a playground of sorts. Adults could play croquet on the front lawn, softball and horseshoe in the orchard.

In the fall, after raking fallen leaves and trimming spent flowers and debris from the garden, we collected a huge pile of leaves to start a bon-fire. We sharpened tree branches to make roasting sticks for the treats of wieners and marshmallows. What a fitting way to end a day of hard labor.

Weiner roast at school

On those summer evenings when it was light until 9:30, we played games on the farm's various lawns. If six or more youngsters were playing, we could play games like those at our small country school.

A game of hide-and-go-seek could be played. Hiding at the approach of dusk made it more exciting even though we'd have to contend with the mosquitoes and lightening bugs that made their appearance at the same time. Two of our favorite games were stealing sticks and prisoners' base.

CAROL: *When I was about seven, we were playing Prisoners' Base at Uncle Edward's home. I tripped, fell under the tree, and broke my collarbone.*

I sat between Mom and Uncle Edward in Uncle Edward's truck and cried as we traveled twelve miles to the doctor's office. The surgeon advised, "Surgery will be needed to mend the break. The fractured bones will be wired together." I remember that whenever the anesthesiologist placed the ether cone over my nose and mouth, the dreadful smell made an image in my mind of a metal cylinder winding round and round.

When I awoke after surgery, I asked Mom for water. She told me the doctor's orders, "You are not allowed

*to drink water right now. It will make you throw up."
Mom patiently stayed near me as I went in and out of
sleep.*

*For ten days, until the day of my release, I lay on my
back with my arm locked into place outstretched at a
90-degree angle. I sat up slowly. But when I hopped
down from the bed, I nearly fainted from weakness.
Again, Mom was there to catch me and hold me until I
got my equilibrium.*

*After a couple of months, the collarbone healed, but
because I was wearing bib overalls with straps over
my shoulders and rubbing my skin, the knot of the wire
holding my collarbone in place crept to the surface of
my skin. The doctor sent me to a specialist in the Twin
Cities for a second surgery to have the knot cut away.
Again, Mom accompanied me on my first train ride—
probably a first for her, too.*

Our cats became our babies as we playd with a ratty old
brown wicker buggy with big, skinny wheels. After dressing
our babies "to the nines," we played "going-to-town" as we
pushed the buggy down the lane toward the fields and back
again.

Wesely cousins with Grandpa and Grandma Wesely; note buggy

78

Our family didn't go on camping vacations, but sometimes it felt like we were camping out in our front yard. At times when we were too warm to go to bed we stayed out on the lawn overnight. We watched the fireflies dance and waited for the stars to slowly appear. If extremely lucky, we could see a great show of shooting stars or the Northern Lights dancing across the sky.

The wide-open sky above the lawn fascinated us. Some cool summer evenings, we stretched out on blankets to gaze at the stars. We recognized and identified a few constellations. Some afternoons after completing our chores, the clouds caught our attention. We told of objects or animals we saw in their mysterious, ever-changing formations.

The lawn was almost completely free of mosquitoes, flies, and gnats in the summer. With the lawn grass cut very low and dried out with summer heat, the bugs stayed elsewhere. Insects are smart enough to hide near cool grass and water puddles. Without insects to sting, bite and generally irritate us, we could spread an army blanket or, even better, an old handmade quilt (which was cooler than those sturdy woolen army blankets) on the lawn for a soft place to sleep.

Cathy, six years younger than Rose and three years younger than Carol, was always the inquisitive, fearless child who explored everything.

One day when Cathy was three or four, she wandered out of Mom's sight and no one could find her. With dangers of speeding cars on the nearby highway, moving farm equipment, the possibility of harm from farm animals, and cornfields six feet high, Mom had reason to worry. Just as panic reached its peak, the three-year-old was found under the swing in the orchard. She was sound asleep, lying on her back with knees raised. She knew how to play hard and sleep soundly wherever and whenever she chose.

Carol found that a lawn could also provide a sense of security.

CAROL: *When I was about ten, I was left home alone with our dog Teddy while the rest of the family was off somewhere. That day, our house, which usually felt warm and friendly, became spooky. I began imagining that an evil stranger or a gypsy was lurking behind all the many doors to our house.*

So with a child's logic, I went outside where I thought I'd be safer lying on the lawn. Resting on an army blanket and a pillow, I felt safe as I stretched out with Teddy beside me. It didn't occur to me that he was worthless as a guard dog. He would have happily licked the face of anyone who came near.

THE HOUSE

A long screened-in porch shaded the living room and front bedroom from morning heat and kept the rooms relatively cool, something we really appreciated in those days before air-conditioning.

However, sitting on the front porch on an afternoon was a luxury not often enjoyed by farm families. But we did use it as a "sleeping porch" in the summer. We'd move a black iron cot with its mattress out onto the porch so we girls (sometimes with one of our parents) would get to sleep much cooler than we would have in the house, which held all the heat of the day. Because the porch was screened on all three sides, Minnesota's notorious mosquitoes couldn't bother us as we slept. So we could sleep away and enjoy the coolness and an occasional breeze.

Summer picnic in backyard; note attached woodshed and iron cot

The front room door leading out to the front porch was not usually used as an entrance. However, the door often stood open on warm summer days for ventilation.

Our family took naps after lunch because Dad enjoyed a noon nap to ease his back pain. Other families also took naps due to the high temperatures and no air conditioning. The household became quiet. In the summer heat, Mom would lie down on the carpeted floor in the cool front room and enjoy the cool breezes off the porch and windows. She'd say, "My back prefers a hard surface."

Other than for naps, the front room was rarely used except for some visits from friends or for Christmas celebrations. The front room (it wasn't called the living room in those days—but we didn't call it the parlor either) was reserved for special occasions. A scratchy brown horsehair sofa, a rocker, and an oval mahogany table furnished the room. A beautiful upright piano was placed against an inside warm wall with the kitchen on the other side of the wall. It was not placed against an outer wall since there could be sudden cooling and a collection of moisture that would affect the tone of the piano and result in the need for tuning—always very expensive. If treated right, the upright piano held its tuning for several years.

Mom relaxed when she played the piano. She'd buy sheet music for popular songs of the day. We loved their decorated front covers. She quickly memorized her favorite hit songs of the day. "When the Moon Comes Over the Mountain" became a favorite song, especially when Dad or Grandpa Wesely could be coaxed to accompany her with the violin or fiddle. The rest of us enjoyed singing along.

Rose: *Many of Mom's siblings played musical instruments; they especially liked playing old-time dance music. Sometimes these musicians played with a band at the Monterey Ballroom near our home. If lucky, we could accompany our parents to wedding dances of neighbors or relatives. There we'd visit and dance feeling ever so grown up.*

Grandpa Wesely and Mom

The open space in the middle of the living room was a perfect spot to set up a card table for card games enjoyed with relatives or neighbors. The card table was set up in the middle of the room directly beneath the only grilled heat vent or register to the upstairs bedroom. If the games continued late into the evening, we girls were sent to bed. This certainly didn't stop us from staying awake, crouching over the open register and looking and listening to laughter and stories from below. Dad was always an excellent story teller and others might tell a tale or joke that smaller ears were not supposed to hear. It was secretive and fun—until we laughed. Then we would hear Dad warn, "Girls, get to bed, right now."

A maroon wool floral-patterned area rug covered the front room's oak floor. In addition, Mom's home-made braided rag rugs covered areas near the door and added warmth. During the long winter months, she made braided rugs from old clothing. Nothing was wasted. The old clothes were torn into three inch strips, sewn together at the ends and then rolled into rag balls. Mom folded under the raw edge of the strips as she braided. The heavy braids would coil in a heap at her feet. Great lengths of braid were required to complete one rug. Mom selected pleasing color combinations before starting to stitch these braids together. She coiled the braids around and around on the floor in the size and shape she chose for each round. She stitched the braids together with a large needle and heavy cord. These braided rugs lasted for many years.

Our kitchen, an open large room in the 1950s, would no doubt be called a great room today. Not a lot of farm life took place in the front room. Farm life meant working outside and getting dirty. Fortunately, we had a portion of the kitchen, like a mudroom, where we could hang up our jackets.

The mudroom, located at the left as we entered the kitchen, had a small shelf that held a small sink with a pump next to it. Two shelves rested on either end of a low cabinet, which held a long narrow sink. On the right-hand shelf, a hand pump brought in soft water from the cistern near the house. The sink held a small enamel bowl for washing up. Shoving the wash bowl to one side, we could place a pail under the pump. When we pumped water into the house from the cistern outside, the water didn't come up on the first down-stroke. It needed priming. We pumped the handle up and down until water trickled and then flowed into the pail.

Before we had an indoor bathroom, this was our small grooming area. In the corner next to the sink a small shelf held a cup of tooth brushes, a comb and hairbrush. This multi-purpose sink was where we washed our faces, brushed our teeth, and combed our hair each morning. Dad shaved there, too, using the mirror over the sink. Every Saturday, we all shampooed our hair there, too. Sometimes, Mom could lift one leg at a time up over and into the sink to wash her feet. This was time-saving. She did not need to fill the wash pan and move it out onto the floor to wash away the mud clinging to her feet after working in the garden. Oh, to be so agile.

An enamel bucket filled with cold drinking water was

carried in from the milk house and placed on the left-hand shelf. Everyone drank water from the same long-handled common dipper. A sink drain removed the water from the house to flow down the hill towards the field lane, keeping the area near the house nice and green.

While we usually washed our hands and face in cold water at the sink in the mudroom, we preferred hot water for some tasks. After filling a pail with cold water from the pump, we carried it across the kitchen and poured the water into the reservoir at the far end of the wood-burning stove. When the water was hot, we'd bring some of it back to the sink to wash hands, wash hair, or wash a single piece of clothing, like a sweater or a pair of nylons.

On the wall opposite the sink, we hung jackets, caps, and sweaters on hooks. A built-in wooden bench with a cover stood below the coats. Sometimes it served as a storage box for mittens or toys. In the winter, we sat on the sturdy box to put on our boots—the old-fashioned kind with metal buckles. Between the sink and bench, a west-facing window overlooked the farmyard.

> **ROSE:** *I was very young when I saw Grandpa Deml sitting near this window to watch the harvest of wheat. Loads of grain were brought in from the fields and were emptied into the elevator leading up into the granary. By this time, Grandpa was unable to assist with the field work due to extreme asthma, which made it difficult for him to breathe. Even walking winded him quickly. That is my last memory of Grandpa as he died shortly afterwards.*

The hot afternoon sun poured in through this same kitchen window. Mom darkened the kitchen by drawing down all the kitchen shades to keep the room as cool as possible during the hot, humid days of summer. When we had measles, Mom set up the black iron cot for us to be near her in the kitchen, darkened the room, and kept an eye on us while she went about her other duties.

This all-purpose corner of the room, sometimes solemn and provoking, often a grooming area, and frequently a small mudroom changed yet again when the grown ups relaxed.

For a little while, a parakeet's cage stood to the left of the sink. The lovely bird sang a beautiful song, sat on Dad's finger, and sometimes flew around the kitchen. The parakeet must have been Dad's idea because his mother enjoyed a canary at home where he grew up and later in her home in town. The bird stayed only a short time because Mom didn't like wildlife—bats, mice, birds, lambs, cats, or dogs—in the house. The house was a place for family members, not pets that created still more chores.

Mom and Dad, with their guests, played cards at a card table set up in the kitchen in order to keep an eye on us small children who used the area as a play corner.

> **CAROL:** *Mother's solemn poker-face usually did not reveal the secrets her cards held. But after she laid down a winning hand, she couldn't suppress a smile. In contrast, when competitive Dad played cards with Uncle Edward and other men friends, we often heard laughter when, in triumph, he slapped down the winning card on the table.*

The kitchen was the busiest room in our house, as it is in most houses. And, while we did a lot of washing up in the mudroom sink, our Saturday evening preparations for Sunday morning began with baths in the kitchen in front of the stove.

Prior to indoor plumbing and—wonder of wonders—hot water from the faucet, we had nice warm water for our weekly bath on Saturday night. The two tables were pulled away and the tub, a large tin five-foot galvanized tub was carried into the room from the back room, where it was stored, and placed directly in front of the stove, close to the water supply and near the heat from the open oven door.

86

In the center of the room, away from drafty doorways, the tub was filled with hot water from the reservoir of the cook stove. The water looked inviting to us. We bathed from the youngest to the eldest with no water changes. We simply added more hot water for each person. The assumption was that the smallest bodies carried the least dirt. This left the water clean enough for adults to bathe in later. After we climbed out of the tub, Mom enfolded us in a large warm bath towel and quickly rubbed us dry.

Then Mom washed our hair at the mudroom sink, dried it thoroughly by rubbing it with a heavy towel, and carefully rolled our hair in twists of white cotton fabric. The rag-rolled curls were soft for sleeping and so pretty Sunday morning when combed into locks.

ROSE: *The Saturday evening routine was incomplete unless Mom prepared us spiritually as well as physically for Sunday morning. We sat around the kitchen table, studying for catechism classes. Mom guided us through memorization of each set of questions and prayers for Sunday morning catechism class at church.*

Ever conscious of how we looked, Mom fixed our hair as though we were in a beauty parlor. In fact, one of her dreams had been to become a beautician. If we had a special occasion at grade school or during the two weeks of our summertime "Sister School," Mom prepped our locks by wrapping our long hair with rags the night before the doings. In the morning she removed the rags, combed through and curled the locks around her finger. Our hair had the look of a pro. No one else wore beautiful locks like ours.

Mom continued her hair styling with each of us. When Cathy was young, Mom pulled Cathy's long, dark hair into beautiful French braids. Sometimes Cathy complained the braids were so tight her eyes pulled to the sides. During Carol's high school years, Mom cut, styled and shaped her fine, wavy hair around her face. As we grew older, Mom gave us perms on a regular basis. The permanent treatment smelled awful.

Cathy's French braid

We girls weren't the only ones whose hair she trimmed. Dad's hair was attacked with her barber set. Aunt Marie liked to "exchange" cuts with Mom. Each would sit for the other until every strand of hair was cut and combed just so!

Rose remembers Mom saying that when Mom was thirteen, she wanted to have her long hair cut for the stylish finger wave of the time. And, oh, how unhappy Mom was with the results. Her naturally wavy thick hair was poorly cut and we have a photo that shows the cut. What a good reason to learn to cut hair properly.

1925 Wesely family photo: Back: Grandpa and Grandma, Eddie, Leona; Middle. Mom (with bushy haircut), George, Martha and Mary, Tony; Front: Robert, Mag, Henry

The wood stove that provided hot water for our Saturday night baths was the most important "appliance" in the kitchen. As the name implies, it was fueled by wood. We carried wood from the woodshed in through the back room and deposited it in the wood box, which stood behind the stove. To put wood in the stove, we lifted the stove's long rectangular lid with a special lid lifter with a coiled steel handle. When the lid was lifted, we could drop in foot-long pieces of split wood into the grate of the stove.

After using the lid lifter, we hung it on the back of the stove. The lifter was also used to lift circular steel plates from the stove top. Setting a pan over this open area provided a quicker, more direct heat. For example, we put the cast iron skillet directly on the opening to provide a higher temperature to fry chicken. As the stove cooled, a soup pot remained off to the right side to simmer in preparation for the next meal.

The burning wood spread heat under the top of the stove and around the oven. Finally, the heat reached the water reservoir and heated water. In addition to hair washing and weekly baths, we used the hot water for washing dishes and doing laundry.

We were forever carrying wood from the woodshed into the kitchen to keep the cook stove going. It took two or three armloads to fill up the wood box behind the stove where we stacked the wood neatly. We had to fill the wood box several times every day.

The stove heated the kitchen and warmed us when we came in from the cold. In the wintertime when our feet felt frozen from doing outdoor chores, we sometimes came inside teary-eyed from the cold. Mom was ready and waiting with an open oven door. After removing our heavy winter coats and boots, we sat down before the stove, removed our shoes and socks, and propped up our feet on towels placed on the oven door, grateful for the heat. As our feet warmed up, Mom gently rubbed them to make the blood circulate.

Behind the stove, a round black six-inch circular pipe attached to the stove extended upwards, then curved just below the ceiling until it reached the chimney which was located between the upstairs and living room doorways. Smoke, soot, and heat traveled through the aluminum pipe to escape up and out the chimney.

During spring housecleaning, the long stove pipe was removed and carried outside for a thorough cleaning both inside and out. This was an important safety measure: clogged pipes and chimneys were often the cause of chimney fires and even house fires.

> **ROSE:** *Once a chimney fire became so fierce that it burned down a neighbor's home. All night long Dad watched until the home was nearly burned to the ground before coming home and waking me. He drove me to the site. In the early light of dawn, only a few flames still licked at the shell of our neighbor's home. By then, most of the gathered neighbors and friends had left the scene. Only a few feet of the shell of the home remained. To impress safety at all times, Dad showed us the hard side of life—but didn't make us watch the most gruesome parts, like the fire itself.*

On the wall behind the mudroom, an enclosed space—actually a small room similar to the mudroom—existed. On two sides, the pantry was lined with bottom cabinets, a counter top, and high cabinets. We entered the pantry from the main part of the kitchen through an archway—there may have been a door here at one time—which faced a window on the west wall. The cabinets held cooking and baking ingredients, cutlery, measuring spoons, knives, pots and pans, and everyday dishes and silverware. On one wall hung two large round pans used for washing and rinsing dishes after meals.

A built-in hinged, fold-out wooden box extended from the floor to the counter top. This triangular container held 50 pounds of flour. Mom used lots of flour for baking bread—four loaves at a time—two or three times a week.

We loved the yeasty smell when we arrived home, especially if the after-school bread treat was covered with sweetened tomatoes or red ripe strawberries fresh from the garden and topped with heavy cream.

Sponge Method: White Bread:

(4 loaves baked in 7½" x 3½" x 2¾" pans)

To make the sponge, measure into a bowl: 3 C. lukewarm water and 4 T. sugar. Sprinkle or crumble in: 2 pkg. of yeast. Let stand until dissolved (5-10 minutes for dry yeast).

Add and stir in: 5 C. sifted all-purpose flour. Beat until smooth. Cover with clean towel. Let rise in warm place, free from draft, until light and spongy, about 1 hour.

To make the dough: Scald 2 C. milk. Add and stir in: 4 T. sugar, 2 T. salt and 6 T. shortening. Cool to lukewarm.

When sponge is light, stir it to break the large bubbles and add the lukewarm milk mixture.

Add and stir in an additional 10 C. sifted all-purpose flour (about). Turn dough out on lightly floured board. Knead 10 minutes. Place in greased bowl; brush lightly with melted shortening.

Cover with clean towel; let rise in warm place, free from draft, until doubled in bulk, about 1 hour and 15 minutes; punch down and divide into 4 equal portions.

Shape into loaves and place in greased bread pans. Cover with clean towel. Let rise in warm place, free from draft, until doubled in bulk, about 1 hour. Bake in moderate oven at 400° F.—about 50 minutes.

91

A space between the top of the cabinets and the ceiling sometimes stored a freshly-baked cake—hopefully, out of reach of touching, tasting fingers. Mom told us that three-year-old Cathy climbed everything, especially in the pantry. Mom would get exasperated and send Cathy outdoors to "help" Dad.

For quite a few years all of our cooking and baking was done on or in the wood-burning kitchen stove. After ten or so years, the pantry also held a new gas stove. It was much better for cooking, and we didn't have to constantly feed it wood.

ROSE: *Dad eventually purchased a small gas stove and placed it in the pantry in front of the window between the cabinets. Even though the space was confined around this stove—barely offering breathing room—we appreciated this model over cooking on a hot wood-burning stove because the wood stove provided an "iffy" oven temperature. Although I never mastered food preparation on the wood cook stove, I found cooking and baking much easier with the modern gas range.*

We made one special recipe in the winter months. Whew. Hot fingers. Do you recall the fun and danger of making pulled taffy? Butter your hands and move swiftly so hot candy does not burn you. Pull and twist and watch the color change. It gets lighter. We rarely wrapped it, but most people wrapped taffy in waxed paper and twisted the ends.

<u>Vinegar Taffy:</u>

Combine in saucepan: 2 C. KARO syrup, 1 T. vinegar, 1 C. sugar and 2 T. butter. Bring to a boil over medium heat, stirring constantly until sugar dissolves. Continue boiling to hard ball stage (260° F.) or until a small amount forms a hard ball in very cold water.

*Remove from heat. Stir in: ¼ tsp. baking soda and 1
tsp. vanilla.*

*Beat until smooth and creamy. Pour into buttered pan.
When cool enough to handle, pull with fingers until
satiny and light-colored. Pull into long strips ¼" in
diameter. Cut into 1" pieces with scissors.*

Dad's elderly aunt, Aunt Mary Prokopec, who never
married, spent several weeks at a time with relatives, making
the rounds. New mothers and busy moms welcomed her
gratefully. She babysat, entertained the youngsters and did
all the mending—by hand or on the treadle (peddled by foot
with no electricity) sewing machine.

Aunt Mary was Dad's mom's sister. Her primary home
was with Grandma. She served as a nanny (today's term),
and moved from home to home helping wherever she was
needed the most. Aunt Mary was short with a very long gray
braid of hair and seemed a bit frightening to youngsters who
did not know her well. No doubt the fear was associated with
the scary bedtime stories she told us. Rose recalls eagerly
awaiting the next story she'd weave for us. Rose kept pulling
the covers tighter and tighter as the story unfolded. Aunt
Mary made up a new scary story each night.

While we loved Aunt Mary, we hated it when she made
breakfast. She didn't cook much at all, except for kushi and
sauerkraut soup.

ROSE: *When Aunt Mary came to stay with us, we
were happy for her other homemaking skills, but she
had few cooking skills. However, she did cook her own
favorite—which no one else liked much. "Kushi," as
she called it, was a hot breakfast soup made from milk
and flour. She sprinkled a bit of sugar over the kushi.
She also made sauerkraut soup—it was edible, but not
necessarily a favorite of anyone else in the house.*

In the kitchen proper, on one side of the archway leading

93

into the pantry, a small drop-leaf table was placed against the wall. When leaves were extended, the table could seat eight people. It was covered with a colorful, floral oilcloth. After lots of use, the colored designs faded, but we kept using it. We always ate our meals together there. A picture of the Last Supper hung on the wall above the kitchen table. Prayer was said before each meal.

Margaret, Alice, Mary and Mom

On the opposite side of the pantry archway stood a refrigerator. It was about four feet tall—the typical size for the 1940s. There was a foot-high electrical unit in the bottom and a two- or three-foot square refrigerator unit with a tiny freezer unit inside. Dad rarely stored a bottle of beer here. Many more bottles could be chilled all at once in the milk house cold water tank.

Two metal ice-cube trays with spring-type handles to release the cubes took up about a quarter of the freezer. A few packages of frozen meat, brought in from our rented locker in town, were packed around a half-gallon box of ice cream. Although we rarely had room for ice cream, trays of ice filled that refrigerator-freezer compartment. We were thrilled to have ice cream year-round instead of churned ice cream only in the winter.

A door separating the refrigerator from the wood stove led into the back room. Because the backroom was not heated, we used it before the holidays as an extra refrigerator and at times a freezer for all the food we prepared for special occasions.

Before neighbors, friends, or relatives—we always said company, never used the formal word, guests—arrived (sometimes with as little as one-hour's notice) or simply dropped in, Mom scurried around washing the floor, cleaning off the daily clutter from the buffet top and dining room table. Then we quickly baked and frosted a cake, made a pan of bars, fixed sandwiches, and brought up a jar of pickles from the basement.

Our visitors—all farmers—were hungry after an evening of cards. Around 10:00 p.m., it was time for lunch and Mom set out sandwiches, bars and cake for everyone. And always coffee! All those goodies were quickly prepared, knowing everyone expected lunch before going home.

Mom loved good food but felt she did not compare to the good cooks that she knew. We knew better. We think of the breads and desserts she made. She certainly had a great collection of recipes! We treasure them still.

Rhubarb Upside-down Cake:

Layer 5 C. rhubarb, cut up small, in a 9" x 13" pan. Sprinkle ¾ C. sugar over rhubarb. Cover with 10 marshmallows, cut in half.

Cream: ½ C. shortening, 1 C. sugar and add 2 beaten eggs. Continue to cream until light and fluffy. Add alternately 2 C. flour, ¼ tsp. salt, 3 tsp. baking powder with ¾ C. milk.

Pour cake batter over the top of the rhubarb mixture. Bake in 350° oven for 60-65 minutes. Serve with cream or ice cream.

Summer picnics, just for family get-togethers or birthdays with family and friends were a special time also.

Deml women: Back: Margaret, Albina, Ag, Mary, Elsie, Babe, Marie
Front: Aunt Mary Prokopec

Mom set the picnic table near the garage and the grove of apple trees across from the house or behind the house under the shade of the elm tree, near the clothes line and gardens. All the delicious food grown and prepared at the farm was most-likely picked and prepared the same day as the picnic. (Farmers' wives did not go to the grocery store or even to their freezers.) Our favorite menu consisted of fried chicken, buttered garden-fresh potatoes, fresh-creamed asparagus, cucumbers in sour cream with fresh dill, and buttered green beans. Dessert highlighted food from our garden: baking powder biscuits covered with home-grown, mashed strawberries and whipped cream, maybe rhubarb upside-down cake with whipped cream from our milk cow, or fresh thick applesauce on crushed graham crackers smothered in thick cream.

If company arrived in the evening, we played a game of whist, buck euchre, 500, or pinochle at the table, and after the game, Mom served a 10 p.m. lunch. Then it was time to do dishes on the kitchen table.

After eating our meals, dishes were cleared and the scraps went into a pail and were saved for the dog or pigs. Nothing was wasted. We brought a large dishpan to the table and filled it with hot soapy water from the reservoir. Washed dishes went into a second large dishpan over which we poured scalding rinse water—heated on the top of the wood-burning stove in a heavy teakettle. A second person stood at the table to dry the dishes and put them away in the pantry cupboard just a few steps away.

Carol dries

ROSE: *Mom knew I did not mind washing dishes. So, when it was my turn to wash, she would bring in every dish from the pantry that needed to be cleaned. But this was OK with me because it gave us the opportunity for mother-daughter girl-talk. We had great conversations while doing the dishes.*

Cathy demonstrates

Dishes were always washed in a specific order. Rose helped Cathy prepare a demonstration on safe dishwashing methods. There is a specific order to the task of washing and drying dishes. Therefore, this information was appropriate for a young 4-H member planning a demonstration. The glasses and cups were washed first, followed by the silverware, which had been soaking in warm water, the plates, the casserole or serving bowls, and finally pots, pans, and greasy containers.

> **CAROL:** *Sometimes when doing dishes, Cathy amused us with some crazy story. When one of us started to titter, we were soon all holding our sides with laughter. Cathy was always good at making us laugh. It didn't have to be anything in particular—just her contagious giggle—and we were off.*

When serving threshing crews or a crowd, we changed the dishwater two or three times. Soapy water was carried out and poured onto plants as a type of fertilizer. It also killed insects on plants.

The rinse water, now at dish-washing temperature, was reused in the dishwashing pan. More dishes were washed and again rinsed with scalding water. After the final rinse over the pots, pans, and freshly-washed greasy containers, we used the rinse water to wash the linoleum floor covering. Recycling was a way of life.

Yes, the kitchen table had multiple uses one of which we would like to forget. You remember that Dad set up the spring fryer business. Well, it was at this everyday table— pulled away from the wall with both leaves extended— where we did our work. After Mom had scalded the chickens in the copper kettle on the gas stove and pulled off the hot feathers, we girls were seated around the table to clean, gut, and pick pinfeathers. Sometimes radio stories helped divert our minds from the yucky task of cleaning chickens.

As we cooked or washed dishes, we sometimes listened to the radio. Ours sat on a shelf above a heat register that blew heat into the room from the furnace below. We listened to the radio for hours.

The music from the radio—old-time music of waltzes and polkas—lightened our housework by soothing our minds and quickening our actions. We could clean house, sweep, and dust while listening to the radio. If we were not outside cleaning the chicken house on Saturday mornings, we enjoyed listening to "Story Hour" with Joyce Lemond.

Only three stations were received in our rural area, unlike the 400 plus stations on Dish Network and innumerable stations on Sirius radio.

Listening to radio station KDHL of Faribault, Minnesota, we listened to weather reports and news of grain and stock market reports. Buying and selling farm products was both a gamble and a business. The weather always affected the markets and, thus, the farmer's economic prospects.

After checking out the weather and stock market reports, Dad changed the station to WNAX, Yankton, South Dakota, for fun and relief with polka music of the ever-favorite Whoopee John. Lawrence Welk was also popular in that era and he lived in North Dakota. Occasionally, a family could afford to have Lawrence Welk play for a wedding dance. Who knew he would become a music icon?

Our third radio station, WCCO, Minneapolis, Minnesota, put the farm families to bed each evening. Everyone recognized the voice of Cedric Adams, the 10 o'clock news broadcaster. Around the country, lights went out with the end of the news. Even airplanes flying overhead realized what time it was when the city below darkened.

On the same shelf as the radio sat a hand-wound alarm clock—the only clock in the house, until the day Rose won a clock radio in a writing contest. This second clock was upstairs in Rose's bedroom.

Around the corner from the radio, hanging on the wall, was a telephone. Our telephone number was 857-L-4. A black box had a speaker pipe that stuck out at adult height.

In those days, we were on a "party" line. Whenever we heard four short rings, we knew that call was for us. The other three families who shared our party line were assigned a special ring: some had two long rings, or one long and two short, or some other variation. While all phone rings were heard in all four houses, we were supposed to answer only when we heard our family's special ring.

However, if we were overly curious, we could pick up the phone and listen in to the other conversations, or even join the conversation. It was not polite but could be helpful (or just plain entertaining) to know what was going on, especially if there was a neighborhood emergency.

> **CAROL:** *When the telephone rang, I'd rush to answer it. Who knew? Maybe it was one of my boyfriends. Wishing. Hoping. Dreaming. Once, I burst from my chair, arms flung out, rushing to beat Rose who was also hoping to answer the phone. My left arm caught her at eye level and tossed her glasses to the floor with a tinkle of broken glass. (The lenses were brittle glass back then unlike today's fairly durable ones.)*

We could call someone on our line by simply cranking the phone handle to make the long and short rings. To call outside our party line, we needed to reach the operator. We picked up the receiver and listened. If our party line was in use, we could hear the conversation, hang up, and try later. If necessary, we would ask for the line and the other party would hang up and the operator would say, "Number, please."

The telephone was necessary and mainly used for emergencies, rarely just for conversations. We were not allowed to talk on the phone extensively or just chat.

> **ROSE:** *I recall a very difficult geometry problem in my evening homework. I interrupted a neighbor's conversation and requested permission to call a geometry student from my class for an explanation. Permission was granted and the problem was solved.*

Near the shelf holding the clock and radio we could look out the kitchen window onto the side porch. We had a good view of the driveway and orchard lawn, should anyone stop

100

to visit or need help. But first they had to pass Teddy on the top step. Now Teddy, our lovable farm dog, found his way into many family photos. Noting his lame front leg, we were reminded of the danger of living close to speeding traffic on the highway. Dogs love to chase cars and, of course, they never win: they are often injured or killed. Teddy learned his lesson—but at least he kept his life.

Carol, Rose, Teddy, Cathy; note Teddy's lame leg

ROSE: *While our family napped, Teddy also slept, as near the family as possible, in the sun's warmth on the steps of the side porch. One day, Teddy was startled by an unexpected visitor. A teenage school friend rode in on her bicycle. She jumped off her bike, threw it on the grass and joyfully ran towards the house, awakening and startling Teddy. He jumped up on her in surprise and knocked her down into the graveled driveway. He then paused patiently by her side, waiting for the family to come outside. She was frightened, scratched by hitting the gravel when she fell, but not hurt.*

Just as our lawns and the highway attracted our attention, it was also an attraction for our dogs. Every dog wants to chase passing cars. If a dog was missing, we assumed the worst. The dog has been chasing cars again and this time has been hit.

Our farm was never without a dog. After our collie Teddy died, Stinky arrived. A handful of wriggling excitement welcomed us as we walked into the yard from country school. She jumped into our arms and licked our faces. Experiencing an exuberant hello made coming home a delight.

Rose holding Stinky; Grandma Deml, Cathy and Carol

CAROL: After a few years of happiness with Stinky, suddenly she no longer appeared. Dad said, "Either she's been picked up along the highway or been run over." We were miserable with this news.

Several years later, while visiting a neighboring farm we saw a youngster holding a perky dog. When we left, I said, "Dad, he was holding Stinky."

"I know," he replied with compassion and understanding for our sadness. "Let's be happy Stinky has a good home and makes the boy happy."

102

Our one-room kitchen included the mudroom, the pantry, the cook stove, the refrigerator, the kitchen table—and the dining room furniture. Our kitchen did not have a separate dining room. On the other end of the kitchen from the kitchen table was our beautiful dining room table.

Mom appreciated her few pieces of fine dining room furniture: matching dining table, chairs and buffet. The oak dining room set—table, chairs and buffet—could be rearranged in this room.

At Christmas time and other special occasions, we set the table using Mom's cherished, seldom-used wedding gifts: crystal glassware, wedding china, and silver-plated silverware, which were otherwise stored in the buffet along with formal linens and napkins.

The oak dining room table, which stood at the end of the kitchen nearest the living room, was multi-functional. The table top held laundry waiting to be folded or already folded ready to be carried to the bedrooms. Serving as a desk, the oak table also held pencils, pens and paper for farm bookwork and school homework.

> **ROSE:** *After school, I stood by the tall oak table as if it were a counter minus stools and read the local daily newspaper, funnies (or comics, as they were called) first, and then the news.*

Sewing projects were spread on the table. Mom was not fond of sewing clothing. She did make herself a few dresses, but bought most of her wardrobe. Although she had very little money, the dresses she bought were of high quality and classic design—so she always looked beautiful. Other family members said that Mom was the best-dressed of all the five girls in her family.

103

Mom and Rose

Feed sack housedresses were common as women's apparel. We used flour sacks as fabric for many things we sewed; they were inexpensive, plentiful, soft, and beautiful for our sewing. We saved the cotton sacks from fifty-pound bags of flour. We bleached the white ones and made them into pillow cases or dish towels. However, if we were lucky Mom always picked lovely colored feed sacks; then, we fashioned the pretty prints into clothing: dresses and sewing projects were spread on the table.

Women wore dresses throughout the year—even in the wintertime, when cotton or nylon stockings (not pantyhose) warmed women's legs. Rubber-buckles on girdles were attached to stockings to hold them. The girdle also firmly held the tummy and buttocks, hopefully restricting bulges. No slacks for women in that era. Actually, cotton dresses or slacks are cooler than jeans. Dresses were protected by aprons. This meant less laundry.

CAROL: *I remember Mom with a half apron tied at the waist and worn over her housedress, covering her from the waist down. Full aprons, which she preferred to wear when working outside or in the garden, covered her entire front. The apron was always handy to lift to carry things, and Mom might gather apples or cucumbers and carry them in the folds of her apron. She quickly removed the apron when someone came to the door.*

*She kept a handkerchief stuffed in her apron pocket—
ready to catch her sneezes: one..., two..., three,...
achoo!—and to wipe our noses when we were little.*

Those feed sacks were also used to make the softest dish
towels and pillowcases. Some of them are still in our family
today. These projects involved crocheting on the edge of
pillow cases and embroidering with embroidery floss or
painting with fabric paints to make the beautiful designs
on the towels and pillowcases. Sometimes we stacked the
fabric paints or embroidery threads before us on the dining
room table in preparation for an afternoon's craft session.

ROSE: *We decorated both dish towels and pillowcases
with either embroidery stitches or fabric paint. For
example, a dish towel with a picture of wash tubs had an
accompanying verse which said: Monday is wash day.
The list continued: Tuesday we iron, Wednesday we
sew, Thursday we market, Friday we clean, Saturday
we bake, and Sunday we rest. Seems they forgot all the
other things we had to do daily, but women did follow
much of the listed routine.*

One particular Lenten season, the buffet was moved to
the other side of the room.

CAROL: *We had decided as a family to go to church
to pray the Stations of the Cross each Friday evening.
One Friday, Dad did not arrive home in time to take
us to church. Mom sat us down in that empty space
on the floor where we took up our books and prayed
without him.*

Another Lenten season, we resolved to pray the Rosary
as a family each evening.

CAROL: *We knelt on the kitchen floor, leaned against
our wooden kitchen chairs and prayed. Oh, oh, we*

105

heard the sound of someone passing gas and we all, Mom included, got the giggles. Dad frowned at all of us. Maybe he was responsible for the stinky whiff.

WORK AND STORAGE AREAS

Dad's "dressing room" was located in the back room behind the kitchen. This unheated room was simply called the back room. It was mainly used to store things: brooms, jackets, laundry, and crates of peaches, pans of berries, or boxes of cucumbers ready to be canned. In there were the laundry tubs, wringer, and the ironing board before these appliances were moved to the basement once hot and cold running water became available. It was also a dropping-off place for items that were to be carried to the basement, such as a pail of eggs.

In the back room Dad dressed for the day and changed out of his dirty work clothes every day, even in the bitter cold of winter. On the wall were hooks where Dad hung his dirty work clothes. After stripping them off, he'd change into the clean set of clothing waiting for him in an extra tall chest-of-drawers.

The back room was originally rather large; it encompassed the area that later was made into our indoor bathroom. The new bathroom took up over half of the back room. Space was left along the outside wall to create a little hallway leading to the back door as well as to the steps to the basement. Going out the back door, we could go to the clothesline, the garden, and the old outhouse, which we didn't miss having to use.

The outhouse, though very tiny, was a building of major importance. The door could be propped open, but being modest girls we usually closed it. This outhouse had three holes of varying sizes to accommodate users from small to large. Sun shone through the window behind us. We read the funnies, farm magazines, newspapers, or perused catalog pages, later used for the big wipe.

Inside the back room of the house, before indoor plumbing, an enamel covered pail substituted for a commode. Coming down from our cold bedrooms in the winter, an evening trip through the backroom to the outhouse was daunting. We certainly preferred the pail to going outside.

We used the outhouse or biffy, as we called it, even after Grandpa and Grandma Wesely gave Mom a large sum of money, which she chose to use to add an indoor bathroom in the corner of the backroom. None of us argued about that decision. The biffy continued in use for many years after the addition of the indoor bathroom because it was quicker to stop outdoors from field or farm work rather than to go into the house.

From the kitchen straight through the back room, another door opened directly into our woodshed, which was attached to the back of the house. The woodshed held wood for the wood stove in the kitchen. The wood was covered from the rain and snow. Hence, it was dry enough to burn well. Although we could have kept it stacked outside under a tarpaulin, it was certainly more convenient not to have to go outside for the wood, especially in our very cold, snowy winters.

The woodshed had another locking door to the outside which we used to bring the wood in after Dad, and any other men helping him, had cut and split the wood into stove-sized pieces. We girls helped carry the wood in from the truck to the woodshed. There we stacked it neatly to make sure we could get as much wood in there as possible. It was an all-day job.

Some memories revolve around strangers, whether on the farm or somewhere else. There were vagrants, hoboes, gypsies and spooky others. Hoboes were moving from place to place, even state to state, looking for work. Sometimes Dad appreciated an extra pair of farm hands, but often they caused troubles big and small. So, it wasn't surprising that our parents told many stories about them, warning us to be very careful around them.

Mom told about the men who came off the train begging for food as she was growing up following the Great Depression during the early 1940s. Her parent's farm was near the railroad. Most of these men were harmless and just down on their luck. Nevertheless, she was also told to stay clear of such fellows. Her mother usually gave a little something to eat to these poor men.

When strangers came to our home asking for food, Dad would occasionally invite the ones he considered honest to work for food. If they stayed overnight, they slept in the barn. Other strangers received a different response.

One day Dad was at home sitting on the woodshed steps cutting up old potatoes which had sprouted to use for spring planting. He had been told about a gypsy (at that time, a gypsy was a traveling individual or family member), who'd stolen food from a Steele Center grocery store after arguing with the owner. While sitting on the steps, a man came up to Dad and asked him something. Dad said, "No." The man, not to be put off, continued to pester Dad. Finally, Dad raised his knife and pointed it at the stranger and said, "I said NO." The man left.

A stranger once approached Carol on the farm (maybe he was one of Dad's helpers), and started doing a weird little dance and singing, "It takes two to tango, two to tango, two to do the dance of love." As he sang and grinned at her, she saw that he was missing some teeth, making him even more scary-looking. She declined to do any dancing.

Besides leading to the outdoor biffy, the clothesline and the back yard, the backroom led downstairs to two large rooms. One was the main source of heat in the winter. The furnace room was directly below our front room and the folks' bedroom. These two rooms had warmer floors than the upstairs bedrooms and were somewhat warm during the cold, windy Minnesota winters. Rooms other than the kitchen (and the front room, if the vent was open) remained cold all winter long.

The furnace room was sufficiently large to store firewood used to fuel the furnace, but first the trees were cut from our grove.

Felling trees is a dangerous business. The yell of "TIMBER!" created a rush to watch a tree fall, but also warned us to stay clear of the falling tree, the trunk and limbs. Sawing and chopping wood were also dangerous. Men worked quickly and the wood pile grew. We helped load wood onto the trailer to haul to the house. The wood chunks for the furnace were large and heavy.

When Dad needed to obtain wood from other sources, he directed and assisted us in loading the heavy stump-like chunks and the cut slabs onto our truck. When we arrived home, Dad backed up to the south basement window, opened it and gave us the job of throwing the chunks down. In the fall, all that lifting, grasping, hefting and throwing made our shirts soaked with rivulets of sweat running down our backs and fronts.

To conserve space, we stacked the wood—from floor to ceiling—in neat rows across from the furnace. Rows and rows of wood were required to stoke the fire all winter long. The job was enjoyable because Dad was there working alongside us.

ROSE: *The furnace and wood were in a room behind a locked door. If a stray mouse found its way into the cellar through the open window and hid in the stacked wood, we did not want the stray finding its way upstairs into the house. Over the years we had very few mice in the house. I believe the mice found the cellar warm and cozy, although I do not know what they ate.*

110

The furnace—a huge monstrosity—took the entire right corner of the furnace room. Because the furnace burned coal along with the wood, the room also was stocked with coal. It was delivered and shoveled through the window down a chute into the coal bin (the alcove into which we had thrown wood now served as a coal bin). While the wood was stacked in the larger part of the room which had cement flooring, the coal remained in the small alcove with a dirt floor. Each winter evening Dad stoked and banked the furnace with coal, in addition to wood, to keep the fire burning all night. Then in the morning, he'd hurry down before the fire died out to fill the furnace with wood.

Not all of the furnace room area had been hollowed out. Opposite the alcove, but at ground level, a shelf the width of the room—about ten feet long—stood about five feet above the basement level, about three feet below the ceiling, and about three feet in depth. Kindling—small branches or finely chopped wood—was stored here to begin a fire in the furnace.

Years later, when the furnace was removed and the house was heated with propane gas heat, the shelf was great for storage. Rose used it to store her shower and wedding gifts. It was clean enough for wedding gifts because Mom had spit-polished and painted the room in her "cleanliness is next to godliness" way.

Rose with wedding gifts

The basement had another room, a multi-purpose room, adjoining the furnace room. It was directly under the kitchen and was a large, spacious area, used for doing laundry, showering, and storing food.

We accessed the basement from inside the house by going from the kitchen through the back room, down the hallway behind the bathroom, through the door—it had a sliding lock on it—and entered the landing. Then we turned right to go down the stairs. Or, we could come in to the landing from outside through the back door—this back door was secured at night with a simple hook and eye closure—and go straight down the stairs. This multi-purpose room was the first basement room we entered and the coolest spot in the house during the summer.

Before one would see the jars, crocks, and barrels of food we stored in the basement, a person would first notice the nice, clean, level floor of the main room of the basement. The stone walls were white-washed and the finished cement floor was painted a soft blue-gray.

The floor was kept so spotless we could eat off it, except for the one time when Lori and a few cousins gathered in the basement, noticed some eggs, and began smashing them on the cement floor. Although the children were delighted with the pretty picture they'd made, the aunts and Mom discovered the mess. The chagrined children left the room while the adults shook their heads and cleaned.

Eggs were stored in the basement year round. In the fall we stored apples from our orchard. Carrots were buried in barrels of sand. Potatoes were gathered into large gunny sacks and stored in the farthest and coolest corner from the furnace room.

We did not grow potatoes on our farm because our large vegetable garden had rich, dense, heavy black soil—not conducive to growing potatoes for winter storage. We traveled to Uncle Edward's farm to plant potatoes. There we found great potato-growing soil—sandy and loose. Each autumn, all of us girls and our cousins were out at Uncle

Edward's potato field picking up potatoes dug by the men folk. Using a large potato fork, or even just a shovel, digging potatoes was a lot of back-breaking work. We picked the quantity we needed for winter use.

ROSE: *A different variety of spuds were planted in our home garden for summer treats of fresh new baby potatoes.*

Crocks standing in one corner held crisp sweet sauerkraut. Fresh sauerkraut, spread with thick cream, was delicious.

Other crocks stored fresh pork in white lard. Fried salt pork, not bacon, was a breakfast favorite. Dad did not have a smoke house to make ham or bacon. Rather, beef chunks prepared in gravy were canned.

The basement was the perfect setting for all the food stored there. The dry cool room had many shelves filled with quart jars of colorful fruits, vegetables, juice, jellies, jams, and canned meat, all prepared by Mom during the summer months. We loved to look at the shelves of canned fruits and vegetables: thick applesauce, sliced pie apples, Bing cherries, California peaches, apricots, strawberries, ground-cherry sauce, and rhubarb, tomatoes, green beans, cucumber pickles—sweet, sour, dill or chutney. Mom did not make catsup or chili sauce. When Mom said, "Go down to the basement, bring up some green beans and some cherries for dessert," we selected from the 350 quart jars she had canned earlier.

No super markets for us. Better yet, our own canned goods were available for a quick meal or lunch—like the TV/ frozen dinners of today. Our meals were prepared almost as quickly and were much tastier and healthier. We appreciated an easy meal after a hard day's work. Our basement held more food than a pantry, refrigerator and freezer combined. During the long winter months, the preserved food provided us with the goodness of summer fruits and vegetables.

When using one of the first pressure cookers, Mom had a frightening experience with an explosion of steam and heat from its boiling hot contents. Thus, she refused to use this faster method for canning. She used a large copper kettle that held fifteen quart jars or eight two-quart jars. The sturdy wood stove could hold the filled weight of the copper boiler. It took many loads of wood to heat that huge container when using the hot-water bath method of canning.

Jars were placed into the boiling water in the canner or boiler, timed, and removed. After cooling the filled jars, they were checked for a complete seal of the lids. The lid of the cover was tapped to listen for a pop. This indicated a seal and it was safe to move the jars to the basement for winter storage.

> **ROSE:** *Modern electric stovetops are not sturdy enough to hold canners or boilers. I tried canning like this for my family but found it less expensive and easier to buy canned food, although I never found them as tasty as home-canned food.*

Before the farm had electricity, we bathed on Saturday night in a tub in the kitchen and washed our hair in the sink with water we pumped. But when electricity came to our farm, many things changed in the house. The improvements included a hot water heater in the basement—and a shower. Dad put the shower and a drain in the northwest corner of the basement. We took off our dirty clothes and put them in the laundry basket, then stepped behind the plastic curtain to shower. It was lovely.

Electricity, an electric water heater, and indoor plumbing eliminated many hours of labor for Mom. An electric washing machine was installed in the basement. Before that, upstairs in the backroom, water had to be pumped and carried from room to room. Even used water had to be carried outside. When the laundry area was moved down to the basement, water came from the hose from a spigot to fill the tubs and waste water went directly down the drain.

Most of the week, the washing machine, wringer, and

double rinsing tubs stood against the wall to the right as we came down the steps. That way, they weren't the first things we saw on entering the room. On Mondays, however, Mom moved everything to the center of the room.

First, we filled up the washing machine with very hot water carried directly to the tubs through a thick rubber hose. All our laundry was washed with Mom's home-made soap. Most farm women in our area made their own soap once a year from the left-over fat that had been carefully saved. (Mom often said that no matter how poor a family might be, they could always afford soap and water. There was no excuse for not being neat and clean.)

The drippings, the leftover fat from all cooked pork and beef, were separated and saved in a crock until soap-making time. The whitest soap resulted from using only the whitest pork fat drippings mixed with Lewis lye. Lye can burn deeply if it falls on the skin, so Mom would never let us near when she was mixing it up. The soap was poured into wooden peach crates that had been saved for that purpose. When it was hardened, we cut it into bars. To wash clothes, we dropped soap chips into the washing machine. This soap was wonderful for washing clothes!

Mom worked hard to make her soap white. (If saved fat was scorched and used anyway, it made a yellowish soap). The neighborhood women seemed to have an unspoken soap competition: The whitest bar always won.

After the clothes were washed in very hot, soapy water, they were wrung out in the wringer three times. The clothes remained in scalding hot water when the washing machine finished washing them—we washed virtually everything in hot water. The clothes were far too hot to be pulled out of the machine by hand. So, Mom (not us kids) would dig them out with a big wooden handle (like a broom handle) and feed the clothes into the wringer piece by piece.

Mom not only didn't want us to be scalded, she didn't want our little fingers near the crushing rollers of the wringer. This first wringing squeezed out the excess hot, soapy water before the clothes dropped into the first rinsing tub, which was filled with hot water. Then, Mom swung the wringer out over the rinsing tubs until it clicked in place over the space between the first and second rinsing tubs. The clothes were taken out of the first rinsing tub, wrung out, and dropped into the second rinsing tub with cold water. Finally, the clothes were wrung out one last time and dropped into a basket. We then lugged the basket of clothing to hang on the clothesline in the back yard.

The wire clothes lines were strung from sturdy poles in our back yard. Before hanging any clothes, we always ran a wet rag over these lines to rid them of dust, dirt and bird-droppings. We secured the clothes on the line with wooden clothes pins pulled out of the clothespin bag, which hung from a hook over the clothes line. We slid the bag along with us as we worked our way down the clothesline. After the clothes were hung, we used long poles to prop the lines a few feet higher up for quicker drying and to keep them (especially the sheets) from touching the ground.

We didn't just hang the laundry helter-skelter: Mom taught us there were two important things to keep in mind. First, we made sure to hang sheets on the outside lines so they would block the view of our more intimate clothing from the people in cars passing by on the highway. Our clothes and underwear were thus shielded on lines behind the sheets. Second, the laundry was pinned with one item right next to another with clothes pins that held the far corner of the first item to the first corner of the next piece of laundry. Socks were the exception to this rule because they took longer to dry.

We hung the laundry outside most of the year. It dried most quickly outside and smelled great! In cold or rainy weather, we hung the laundry in the kitchen.

Contrast clothing dried in summer's sunshine and warm breezes with winter's cold and blustery weather. On those days Mom lined the kitchen with heavy cotton cord strung crisscrossed throughout the kitchen. When we came home from school we'd find clothes hanging all around the room. They dried throughout the day in the warmth provided by the wood stove and furnace. If Mom would have allowed it, it would have been a great place for a game of hide-and-seek. And it was so funny to see Dad's long underwear blocking the door to the front room.

Because Monday was laundry day, Tuesday was the day to iron clothes. One can understand why there were several nursery rhymes and a song or two that started this way, "Monday we wash and Tuesday we iron." Mom used flat irons heated on the top of the stove. Note that this was still before electric steam irons so we had to sprinkle the clothes with water before ironing them.

Laundry was washed, hung on the line to dry, picked and folded. This was before spray bottles, so we cleaned an empty Coke bottle, filled it with water, then capped it with a metal snap-on cover that looked like the top of a salt shaker with large holes in it.

A shirt to be ironed was carefully flattened, sprinkled evenly with water, rolled tightly, and then wrapped in a towel and set aside to give time for the moisture to spread evenly through the shirt. Sometimes during the summer, when the sprinkled clothes might dry out before Mom could get to the ironing, she placed the rolls of ironing in the refrigerator to retain necessary moisture.

Rose recalls the ease and efficiency that electricity brought to our home when Mom could use an electric iron. She tested the heat of the electric iron by moistening the tip of her finger with saliva and then touching the hot iron to hear a sizzle indicating it was the right temperature to create steam when she pressed the shirt.

Steam irons were developed after that! And after that drip-dry clothing—which had to be washed in cold water!

ROSE: *One day when I was ironing with the electric iron, young Cathy was sulking around the kitchen about something or other. She first tried to hang on to*

117

me, but I shook her off. Then Cathy went around the ironing board and, pouting, leaned over it. The iron, which had been sitting on its heel, promptly toppled over onto Cathy's bare arm, leaving a full imprint of the iron on her skin. Fortunately, she was not badly burned, and the incident taught Cathy not to lean on the ironing board. The imprint remains today. I wonder if the incident taught her not to pout.

UPSTAIRS

The master bedroom—always called the front bedroom or Mom and Dad's bedroom—was off the living room. It was the coolest room in the house with north and east facing windows to catch a summer breeze.

There was no door to the bedroom but an opening the width of double doors. Loosely woven brown–gold plaid curtains hung on brown wooden rings at the bedroom's entrance. On warm nights, these were left open for ventilation. Sometimes they were drawn to keep the room cooler than the living room. At other times, they were drawn for privacy.

ROSE: *In the middle of one hot summer night, Mom and Dad were awakened and surprised by a very dazed man who entered the front porch door, the front room door, and then stepped right—into their bedroom. He had rolled his car over onto the lawn, crawled out and walked into the house in a daze. Standing at the foot of the bed, he asked for help. Startled, but ever ready to help, Dad got up, called the sheriff, and assisted the fellow to the scene of the accident. Hours later, after the ambulance departed with the dazed and injured passengers, Dad awakened me and said, "Look out*

119

*your bedroom window." A tow truck/wrecker was
about to turn the stranger's car right side up.*

*Dad taught me about the dangers of careless driving
and explained the helpfulness given by so many service
people. This accident was one of many that happened
on that busy highway in front of our house.*

Mom and Dad had purchased a bedroom set on their
short wedding trip to Minneapolis. Mom selected a beautiful
mahogany set that included several pieces. The bed had a
scrolled, curved headboard.

CAROL: *Sometimes the bedroom was a comfortable
place of relief. Dad's bad legs required rest in the
evenings. On occasion, he would lie down and ask
me—then a youngster—to come into the bedroom
to comb his hair, a pleasant task. Sometimes I also
clipped his toe nails, not an unpleasant task either
because I enjoyed being in Dad's peaceful presence.*

Mom's dresser came with a mirror. Then there was Dad's
tall chest of drawers and the chair. The design on the chair's
back matched the curvature of the headboard and mirror's
frame. Our family treasured this furniture for years.

A lovely wood cross hung above Mom and Dad's bed.
The cross opened and became a sick call set, including
candles and candle stick holders, a bottle of holy water, and
a stand to hold the cross. Should someone have needed the
services of a priest in our home, the sick call set was ready
for use. I don't think we ever used it. However, the fact
that Mom and Dad purchased it for that reason was a faith-
building experience.

Although we were not supposed to be in our parents'
bedroom, it was quite tempting to go in and play and
then check out the pretty things in and on Mom's dresser.
Costume jewelry, a watch, a locket—a gift from Dad—and
lovely lace handkerchiefs lay in the left-hand top dresser

drawer. A silver-plated three-piece dresser set (hand mirror, hair brush and comb) was carefully placed on a long white linen dresser scarf. A hat, a bottle of perfume, a small glass dish and picture also stood on the dresser. It was so beautiful.

Later, there was also a bride doll on the dresser. At a summer festival at St. Ben's, Mom won a doll dressed in bridal clothing. Claiming the doll was the only thing she ever won, she proudly displayed the treasure on her dresser. Another item there was a white glass chicken. A cover—the head, with its red combs above and below the beak, and upper body—lifted to show, in the lower part, a dish to house some jewelry or other treasures.

In their bedroom, Mom and Dad's good clothes hung in a very narrow, deep closet. This tiny closet was directly below the steps leading upstairs. Boxes of out-of-season clothing, winter bedding and other seldom-used items were tucked way back under the steps and under the hanging clothes. The closet walls separated the bedroom from the rest of the main floor of the house.

Our house did not have an entry room with a closet for hanging guests' coats. Instead, when neighbors visited for an evening of card playing, coats covered their beautiful bed. Mixed among the coats, a mom could lay her sleeping baby cuddled deep within a wall of coats. The bedroom opened up into the parlor or front room, as we called it. The families played cards in that room, close to their sleeping children.

We were rarely allowed to go into either the front room or Mom and Dad's bedroom—mainly to keep them free from the dirt on our shoes and clothing. Saturday was the day to clean, both indoors and outdoors.

Outdoors, the chicken house, pig house, and horse barn needed to be cleaned. (When we had dairy cattle, the cow barn was cleaned daily.) Pitching manure is quite different from dusting. But, we were at least rewarded with the smell of the fresh sweet golden straw spread in the cleaned buildings.

When we completed the outdoor chores and the Saturday

121

cleaning of barns and buildings, we returned to the house to dust. Beginning in the front bedroom, we dusted Mom's handsome mahogany bedroom suite. Going from the bedroom to the front room, we dusted the oval end-table, mopboards, piano and piano bench. We used a small push carpet sweeper on the big area rug and gathered all the throw rugs to shake out the dust.

We rolled up area braided rugs from Mom and Dad's bedroom and from the girls' rooms upstairs and carried them outside to shake out the dust. The floors around the front room area rug and the upstairs floors were dust-mopped; the stairway steps were wiped with a damp cloth. Heat from the kitchen wood stove and from the wood- and coal-fired furnace in the basement, and the loose dirt from fields coated everything with dust. There was plenty of dusting to do each week.

> **ROSE:** *The girls' bedrooms were upstairs. On one occasion, I was expected to have the three of us sound asleep when Mom and Dad returned from an evening of card playing at the neighbors. I was unable to quiet the younger girls and put them to sleep. In desperation, I thought it might be a good idea to try something else. I led my two younger sisters into Mom's big bed and started telling them scary stories, hoping the girls would lie very still, cover their heads and fall asleep. Unfortunately, Mom and Dad returned before that happened. They found us giggling and telling stories.*

Near the archway into Mom and Dad's bedroom were two other doors: one led out of the front room into the kitchen and the other upstairs (a door that was usually kept locked). When unlocked, this door revealed a high landing leading upstairs. Movers used this particular living room door for a straight run at getting large pieces of furniture to the upstairs bedrooms without having to make the turn from the kitchen.

Mom would call to us. "Beware of this landing, girls. You could fall and hurt yourselves." We loved it when the door was open because then we could jump down into the living room. Visiting cousins really loved this jumping-off place into the living room until Mom found us, chased us away, locked that door and stopped the fun.

On the landing and before climbing the upstairs steps, we took a left turn and two steps down into the kitchen. These steps, used daily, led from the kitchen to the upstairs.

CAROL: *Dad stood at its base each morning, calling each of us to arise. In icy wintry weather, I didn't want to touch my feet to the cold floor. Pretty soon, Dad would call again. The third time, I scrambled at the sound of his booming bass voice. With blurry eyes and scowling face, I stumbled into the kitchen. He looked up, cap on his head, grinned and greeted me, "Good morning, Sunshine."*

Walking up to the second floor, a window a bit off to the left provides a view of the backyard, clotheslines, and outhouse. At the top of the steps, we could stop to look out the north window high above the lawn. This gave us a tree-house view of the leaves on the magnificent box-elder tree waving in the breeze. Making a U-turn around the newel post and railing, we entered a triangular hallway as we approached three small bedrooms.

There was a triangular guestroom on the left of the hallway. Windows on the north and east provided light in the bedroom. Above the bed, at the wide end of the room, hung a picture of a calm, composed woman holding a sleeping baby. Her tender gaze symbolized all things good and holy. We wonder whatever happened to the oval framed picture.

At the narrow end of the room, the view of our front lawn from this high up was a great place to daydream. Mom's cedar chest, a gift from her parents with her initials EW (Elsie Wesely) on the front, stored her own embroidered towels, some of her mother's hand-crocheted doilies, and other treasures. The cedar chest was filled with beautiful linens and one incomplete quilt top with roses appliquéd by her mother, Rose Wesely, as her wedding gift to Mom.

CAROL: *I cherish the times Mom allowed me to come with her to explore the depths of the cedar chest.*

Past the guest room, Rose's bedroom—the largest of the three—had a window to look over the front lawn and across the highway to the fields east of our farm. The south window overlooked the apple orchard, the driveway, and farm activities.

ROSE: *My mirrored dresser had three deep drawers. A metal triangular bar over the door held my complete wardrobe—two dresses, one overcoat, three cotton skirts, and two white Peter Pan collar blouses. I could vary the appearance of this wardrobe for school by wearing a different scarf tied around the collar, or one of my three short-sleeved sweaters. A necklace of faux pearls gave more variation to my daily school outfits. Bobby pins and barrettes were my only hair decorations.*

In the dresser drawer I had two pairs of slacks, not jeans. Girls did not wear jeans or even slacks to high school. I even wore a dress the day I showed my 1,000-pound baby beef steer at the county fair. Few teenage girls wore slacks or jeans unless they were working on the farm.

My shoe collection consisted of black and white saddle shoes, brown penny loafers, and black patent slip-on shoes stored under the foot of my bed. Slightly small and very worn shoes were kept on the porch for chores and outdoor work.

Teenagers tried to dress like movie stars of the day. Grace Kelly and Doris Day were two of my favorite movie stars. I saw very few movies. "Song of the South" and "Lassie Come Home" were two of my favorites.

Once a year, live performers came to Owatonna's Roxy Theatre. Dad especially enjoyed the music and ventriloquist. I felt quite rich when I could attend this event in town. It was living high for a country girl.

Rose's dresser faced the bed stuffed in the corner of the room. A small table near the south-facing window held the clock radio Rose won after entering a writing contest sponsored by the town's radio station. We liked to listen to programs at night before sleep overtook us.

Cathy

One of Rose's favorite prayers was the Prayer of St. Francis:

Prayer of Saint Francis of Assisi

Lord, make me an instrument of your peace.

Where there is hatred, let me sow love;

125

Where there is injury, pardon;

Where there is doubt, faith;

Where there is despair, hope;

Where there is darkness, light; and where there is sadness, joy.

O Divine Master, grant that I may not so much seek

To be consoled as to console; to be understood as to understand;

To be loved as to love.

For it is in giving that we receive;

It is in pardoning that we are pardoned;

And it is in dying that we are born to eternal life.

ROSE: *I kept a copy of St. Francis' Prayer by my bed. Mom told me that when she first saw it there and read it, she cried. She was aware of her bipolar illness but could not control her changes of mood and recognized that it affected her children. The sentiments in the prayer embodied her unexpressed plea for God's help.*

In this bedroom, a grate on the floor (called a register) allowed heat to rise from the living room below. In summer, we kept it closed so the hot air would not rise. In winter, we were happy it opened to let the warm air into the room.

The third bedroom at the end of the hallway had only a single window facing the driveway and orchard. The room seemed larger than Rose's room. The extra space allowed Carol and Cathy to rearrange the bed and dresser for folded clothing. None of the bedrooms had closets. Ironed clothing hung on a triangular metal bar that hung on each bedroom door inside the room.

After Rose went to college, Carol and Cathy each had a bedroom—but not for long. Dad used the third bedroom because his health required an elevated bed. He chose this room so that he would not disturb Mom's sleep. He propped one end of the bed against a wall and put wooden blocks under the legs at the opposite end. This put the bed at a slant, thus releasing pressure caused by his hiatal hernia.

A door in the corner of this third bedroom opened into the attic, directly above the kitchen. A wooden hand-turned latch secured the door. The attic was the largest room upstairs. It was a long dark room lit by a single bulb hanging from the ceiling and a window opposite the door.

The upstairs with its attic was neither heated nor cooled. The exposed, non-insulated walls of the attic made this room even colder in the winter and hotter in the summer than the three bedrooms. But it at least served as a buffer or sort of insulation for the kitchen below.

Mom stored many things in the attic. An adult could stand in the center under the roof peak but not on the north or south sides where the roof slanted directly down to the floor boards. Boxes of unused or outgrown clothing, Christmas decorations, and odds and ends were pushed back under the rafters. Only a small center portion had flooring. The other areas exposed rafters, making this a hazardous place for children.

ROSE: *The attic was off-limits to children unless an adult was present. Who knew what hidden treasure might be found in one of those boxes? The warning to stay out of the attic made it exciting to sneak in to look at stored items. It was also a place to hide from a visiting cousin or playmate. This also meant it became a source of treasured memories.*

There are more memories associated with the bedrooms. Minnesota has extremely cold winters and brief periods of extreme heat in the summer. Without heat or air conditioning we used windows to provide some relief from the elements. In the summer the bedrooms could be cooled with a breeze or cross breeze from north, south and east windows.

In the winter the same windows were coated with beautiful patterns of ice. We delighted in art created by Jack Frost but were not so thrilled to walk across cold, cold floors. We hurried down to sit by the heat released from the open oven door in the kitchen.

We three girls kept warm in the winter by snuggling together, spoon-fashion, under deep feather quilts and several blankets or quilts. The heavy wool patchwork quilts were made of squares cut from coats and men's suits. Several of Mom's hand-braided rugs lined the hallway. Also, each of the bedroom floors had one or two braided rugs, providing some relief from the cold floors.

CHRISTMAS

While we naturally spent most of our time on the farm, many important parts of our lives revolved around special events not limited to one room or building on the farm or in the house. We enjoyed Christmas vacation with its special celebrations.

Just before Christmas vacation each year, the country school children of District #22 put on a Christmas program. This event was planned for the whole rural community, not just the families of students but neighbors as well. The students eagerly memorized lines and practiced parts for the Christmas play. In music class, we learned Christmas carols that the audience sang with us. The excitement, planning, and preparations extended into students' homes as well. Each family would donate homemade goodies to fill Santa's gift bags. Homemade popcorn balls, fudge, divinity—a fluffy white melt-in-your-mouth candy—and possibly some purchased colorful ribbon candy also went into the bag that Santa presented to each family. Some people brought colored divinity. Mom made white divinity.

Divinity:

Place in saucepan over low heat: 2 c. sugar, ½ c. white corn syrup, and ½ c. water.

Stir until sugar is dissolved and then cook without

129

stirring to a hard ball stage. This stage is reached when the thermometer registers 252°. (Without a thermometer, here is another way to test the hard ball stage. Drop a little of the syrup into cold water. It should form a hard ball or/and it also should form a fine strand that blows away.)

Remove pan from heat and pour, beating continually, in a fine stream over 2 egg whites, stiffly beaten. It is best to use a free-standing mixer; a hand-held electric mixer will overheat. Continue beating egg white/syrup mixture about 4-5 minutes until mixture holds its shape and loses its gloss. Add 1 tsp. vanilla, 1/3 c. finely-chopped well-drained maraschino cherries (optional), and ¼ c. finely-chopped walnuts, (also optional). Drop candy quickly from tip of tablespoon unto waxed paper into small peaks.

Excitement for the school program began with decorating the tree with paper ornaments and paper chains made in art class. Student-drawn and -colored pictures were hung around the room. The older students moved and stacked desks in the library to make room for benches brought up from the basement. That evening the overflow crowd squeezed into the school's one small room that evening. Backstage was the basement stairwell where little ones were asked, "Please, please be quiet so the audience does not hear you."

Our school, District #22, was one of the very few that had a basement. It housed a really huge furnace used to heat the building. It was a neatly painted basement with picnic tables—a place to play in winter when it was too cold to play outdoors.

At last, the nervous and excited children completed the program. Students and children in the audience anticipated the coming of Santa. They sang and awaited his arrival. Santa arrived. He wore black boots and a white beard, carried a pillowcase stuffed with the bags of goodies, and entered the school with a hearty ho-ho and much jingling of bells. What a way to end a wonderful evening and begin Christmas vacation.

At home we prepared for Christmas. We set up the card table in the living room to address Christmas cards and write letters. We used the card table instead of the kitchen or dining room table because the project could remain several nights in the living room with the door closed. If cards had been written on the kitchen table, the cards would have needed to be cleared for meals each night.

The front room, reserved for special occasions, became the center for our Christmas festivities. Only our lovely Christmas crèche was displayed on the buffet in the kitchen where we could enjoy it daily.

A day or two before Christmas, Dad cut a Colorado blue spruce from our grove. Dad placed the tree in its tree stand and centered the tree in the living room—cooler than the kitchen—and the door was often closed to keep it even cooler to make the tree last as long as possible. We watered the tree daily to keep it fresh.

Dad hung several strands of blue electric Christmas bulbs onto the branches, some deep within the branches and others closer to the tips. We decorated our spruce tree with long strands of tinsel, each one hanging straight down on both sides of a branch. Mom allowed no tangles. How the tinsel shimmered when the blue bulbs lit the tree.

Mom and Dad's narrow, deep closet was a great place for Mom and Dad to hide unwrapped Christmas gifts and a common place for us girls to search. Then on Christmas Eve, wrapped gifts appeared under the beautiful tree. One year Rose received a wind-up train set from a neighbor. Dad was soon down on the floor putting it together. He placed the tracks just so, set the engine and cars atop the tracks and watched them traverse the terrain of the carpeted room. Dad was the one who had the best time with that "child's" toy.

Especially memorable were those Christmas Eves when a couple of families joined us for the celebration or we met in their homes. On this special occasion, the dining room table was cleared and covered with a linen table cloth. Now we could use the crystal, fine china, and silver saved only for company. In those days, Christmas Eve was a fast and abstinence day, meaning we could not eat meat. So the main dish was fish—often our favorite deep-fried walleye fillets, caught and frozen the summer before. The table was laden with goodies.

We all enjoyed the special treats but were eagerly waiting for a personal visit by Santa to our home. The families exchanged gifts and played with the new toys and games. All eating stopped at 9 p.m. because of the three-hour fast in preparation for going to Holy Communion at Midnight Mass. After Mass, we returned to the home of the host family for a one-time-a-year wee-morning-hour breakfast.

At each home a family specialty was served on Christmas Eve. Some favorites were frozen pineapple dessert, filled prune and poppy seed biscuits, and homemade pickles, jams, and relishes. Dad's brother, Edward, and his family had several children similar in age to our family. The two families took turns hosting the other family. A few years later a third family, Uncle Henry and Aunt Babe with their children, joined us in this exchange.

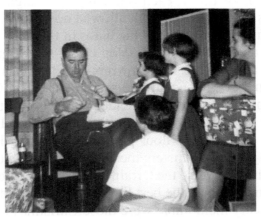

Dad, Sandy, Shirley, Aunt Babe in our front room

One Christmas Eve at our home, following a delicious meatless meal, the opening and sharing of gifts, and a few board games, the families went to Midnight Mass in Owatonna, three miles away. (When we spent the Eve at Uncle Edward's home, we went to Mass at Holy Trinity Church in Litomysl.) The families returned to our house for a bite to eat. Mom hurried out to the backroom to bring in pans of bars and sweet prune-filled biscuits to serve the hungry group so early in the morning.

Then, gifts were gathered up, and Uncle Edward's family was bundled into their car to return to their farm. But, oh my, a blizzard had begun and their farm was eight miles to the south. Plans were changed and Dad hitched the horses to the sleigh—no car could drive through those snow banks drifting across all the roads. Definitely, Uncle Edward's family would stay overnight at our house. However, the men must return home to be ready to milk and feed their large dairy herd the next morning. Dad and Uncle Edward went to the farm by horse and sleigh, and the rest of the family stayed overnight with us. A dairy herd needed to be milked at a specified time. Dad never had that problem because our beef cattle only needed to be fed, not milked.

Usually, Christmas Day was spent at home, relaxing and playing board games, reading or napping after outdoor chores were completed. Three days after Christmas, December 28, on Aunt Mary's birthday, the two families again gathered for winter fun. A large birthday dinner, served at noon, was prepared. Farmers ate noon dinner and evening supper. (Farmers ate lunch at 10 a.m., 3 p.m. and 10 p.m.)

All the cousins were dressed in layers of coats, mittens and scarves, and everyone went outdoors to play in the snow. The little ones made angels in the white fluffy snow. The older ones looked in the garage for the long wooden skis and sleds. A modern ski is much shorter. Long skis were made for hills, but southern Minnesota had no hills. Instead, the skier held on to a thick twisted hemp hay rope tied to the tractor and attempted to ski in the wide ditches beside the highway.

The only thing to stop us was an occasional driveway across the ditch. We tried to ski in the fields. However, the snow layers and ice formations in plowed fields made skiing over these bumps a rough ride. The ditch was the preferred way to go. We learned to water-ski without water.

If not making snowmen, skiing or sledding we tried to ice skate on the frozen slough. Before waters of the slough were drained by tile, the water froze over in the winter. The west winds blew over the freezing water, creating ripples and bumps in the ice. Patches of grain stubble or corn stalks protruded above the ice. This ice pond was not smooth but we loved trying to skate on our rink in the middle of the field.

CAROL: *Someone twirled Cathy round and round on the sled over the bumpy ice. It was great fun until she flew off and went home crying with a fractured collarbone.*

Although we had ice skates, none of us had snow shoes. We tramped through the snow in large boots to do our chores.

Back at the house we were eager to play whist or buck, both card games the adults enjoyed and taught the teens to play. Smaller children played with Christmas toys. Puzzles, spinning tops, wind-up trains, and Lincoln logs covered the floor space.

ROSE: *The card game whist is a forerunner of bridge. If only my Mom and Dad had been introduced to bridge, they would have been champion players. I learned to play whist with them and have since learned to play bridge, have taught party bridge, and now enjoy the challenges of playing duplicate bridge.*

After playing in the snow, everyone was eager to eat lunch once again. Sandwiches, pickles, cake, Christmas cookies, and homemade ice cream were typical treats. Some of the other cousins helped Dad churn ice cream early in the day.

Making ice cream was fun—and quite a bit of work. We made it easily with an ice-cream maker and a recipe based on a cooked custard. First, the custard—that would be frozen into ice cream—was boiled on the stove. Much stirring was required to prevent curdling or too thick a custard. More cream and optional fruit were added to the mixture before pouring it into the canister for churning. The canister was then placed deep within a wooden bucket with a churning handle—our ice cream churn. A mixture of snow and rock salt was packed around the metal canister. The snow melted and ran out between slats.

We yearned for velvety-smooth homemade ice cream. That velvety texture our family loves depends on packing the ice-cream maker with ice and rock salt in the proper proportion so ice melts at a proper rate to freeze the mixture quickly and smoothly. Using too much salt produces grainy ice cream; using too little prevents freezing.

Ice Cream:

Custard: Early in the day: In a heavy, 3-quart saucepan, whisk 6 T. all-purpose flour, 2 C. sugar and 1 tsp. salt.

Blend 5 C. milk and 6 eggs. Then add to ingredients in saucepan and whisk all until well blended. Cook over medium-low heat, stirring until mixture thickens and coats spoon, about 30 to 45 minutes (do not boil). Cover surface with plastic wrap and cool about 2 hours.

Mix 4 cups half-and half (or heavy cream) and 2 T. vanilla extract into cooled egg mixture. Pour into 4- or 6-quart ice-cream-freezer can.

Use about 10 pounds cracked ice and 3 C. rock salt to surround the freezer canister.

135

Layer ice and salt in freezer bucket as manufacturer directs. Fill bucket half full with ice, sprinkle with ¼ C. rock salt or 3 T. table salt. Repeat layers of ice and salt until 1 inch below can lid. Freeze as manufacturer directs, adding more ice and salt. The churning takes 25 to 35 minutes. When it feels impossible to turn the crank, the ice cream will be the consistency of heavy whipped cream.

After churning, ice cream is soft. Remove motor or crank. Wipe lid clean. Remove paddle; with spoon, pack down ice cream. Cover surface of ice cream with waxed paper. Replace lid and put cork in hole in center; add more ice and salt to cover lid. Let stand to ripen—which means giving all the ingredients time to blend—and continue freezing firmly (about 3 hours), adding ice as needed. Or, place container in home freezer for 3 hours. Makes about 4 quarts.

ROSE: *Dad continued to pack more snow and salt as I churned. A slow continuous churn made a smooth ice cream. As the ice cream hardened, it became more and more difficult to turn the churning handle. And Dad would do a final churn just to make it as stiff as possible.*

The churning paddle—dasher—does all the work. The dasher removes the frozen mixture accumulating on the ice cold walls of the canister, breaking up ice crystals and "beating in air" to create a light creamy texture. We always hoped the dasher would be heavily coated with ice cream for us to lick and taste. Who wants to wait for it to ripen or harden?

Approximately 20 minutes were needed to firm the ice cream, and then everyone eagerly awaited the first taste. The beater that stirred the ice cream as we churned would be carefully pulled out and placed on a platter. Quickly grabbing a spoon or even using a finger, we ate off the beater, licking

136

it clean. The canister was closed and wrapped tightly to set for several hours. This period of waiting is called ripening and develops the full flavor.

Some families churned ice cream in a wooden bucket for the festivities on the fourth of July using ice stored below ground and covered with straw. We simply packed snow around the bucket in the winter time and enjoyed our ice cream then.

And, of course, there were also always kolacky. These filled biscuits were a Bohemian specialty. The biscuits were filled with prunes, apricots, or poppy seed. Everyone had a favorite.

CAROL: *I always called this specialty kolacky, but according to definitions from Steele County Historical Society, "kolace" (or our spelling, kolacky) was the plural of "kolacek," which is a smaller version of the kolac. The kolac was an open-faced, round tart with poppy seed or other filling. Kolo was Czech for circle or wheel. The kolac could be as large as a pie. That is not what we prepared.*

We prepared buchty (pronounced book-thee)—the right label for one of my favorite foods—a poppy seed, prune or fruit-filled biscuit. The dough was cut in a square with filling placed in the center. Then the corners were drawn up, placed one on top of the other and pinched shut tightly over the top of the mixture.

Buchty (Kolacky) (Filled Biscuits):

Yeast Mixture: Into 1 cup lukewarm water, add 1 T. yeast and 2 T. sugar. Stir. Let set.

In a separate bowl, add to 1 cup scalded milk, 6 T. shortening (margarine), ½ C. sugar, and 1½ t. salt. Stir in ½ cup flour to scalded milk mixture; beat well.

Add 3 eggs (beaten well) to yeast mixture. Beat well. Mix with scalded milk mixture. Add enough flour (about 7 cups) to make a soft dough.

Knead 8-10 minutes. Let rise 1½ hours. Punch down. Divide into 2 parts. Roll out. Cut into 3 inch squares and spoon into the square a teaspoon of poppy seed, prune or apricot filling, pulling up opposite corners of dough and pinching the dough tightly to close over the mixture. If necessary, grease your pan and place biscuits near one another. Set aside and allow to rise a second time. Bake at 400° for 15-18 minutes.

Poppy Seed Filling:

Grind 1 C. poppy seeds. Then heat them in 1 pint milk. Add ½ C. raisins and a pinch of salt. Stir in 1½ tsp. Cream of Wheat®. (Rose's mother-in-law substituted one egg for Cream of Wheat®.) Cook for 15-20 minutes. Add 1 C. sugar to thin down. Cook for 5-10 minutes. (Don't scald or burn!) One recipe fills 2 dozen biscuits.

Prune/Apricot Filling:

Cook 2 lbs. pitted prunes in a kettle. Prunes should be covered with water. Drain. Mash with electric mixer.

Then add: 1 C. sugar, 1 tsp. cinnamon, and 2 C. thick apple sauce.

(Substitute dried apricots, if you desire, for the prunes. For apricot filling, double the amount of sugar and apple sauce.)

With the advent of electricity, Dad purchased a freezer and placed it in the backroom. One of his favorite desserts was frozen pineapple dessert.

Frozen Pineapple Dessert:

Crumb base: Roll 20 graham crackers very finely. Spread half in the bottom of a 9" x 9" pan.

Egg mixture: Cream: 1 ¼ C. powdered sugar and ½ C. butter. Add 2 eggs and beat until very creamy. Pour half of the egg mixture on the crumbs.

Pineapple mixture: 1 C. cream, whipped stiff. Fold in: 1 C. drained crushed pineapple and ½ C. finely chopped walnuts. Spread pineapple mixture over layers in pan. Cover with the remaining half of the egg mixture. Finally, layer with the remaining crumb base. Freeze for several hours before serving. Serves 9.

Several weeks before Christmas, a great batch of white bread, at least four large loaves, was prepared just to make houska, a braided Bohemian bread filled with walnuts and raisins. Mom usually made houska only at Christmas—probably because houska is less expensive to make than fruit cake—and she made it every Christmas because we all loved it so much. Making houska was quite a production: Mom would mix up the large batch of dough needed, and Rose or one of the other girls would help her braid the three long rolls of dough. The braid was set aside to rise.

After baking, the houska was set in a cool place for the flavors of raisins, walnuts and cinnamon to blend. The flavor developed if made several weeks before eating, but then who could possibly wait that long? On Christmas morning, houska was sliced and toasted in the big cook stove oven, then spread with rich creamy butter. How quickly it disappeared.

Houska: A Bohemian-Czech Christmas Bread:

A hint: There will be two layers of braids (or a total of six strips in each of the braids). There will be two Houskas (or a total of twelve strips).

139

Follow the white bread recipe found earlier in this book, adding 3 C. raisins and 2 C. walnut halves while adding the last 8-10 C. flour. Makes a stiff dough. Let rise until doubled in size.

Divide in 2 portions. Set aside one portion. Hint: One braided Houska will be placed on one cookie sheet. This recipe makes two Houskas.

To shape Houska: Divide the first portion into two pieces. The first piece—2/3 of the dough—is rolled into a long roll about 2" in diameter and cut into 3 pieces for the bottom braid. The remaining 1/3 piece is rolled into a long roll about 1" in diameter and cut into 3 pieces for the upper braid.

Place 3 thick strips on the cookie sheet and braid the first layer, sealing under at ends. Place 3 thinner strips on top and braid the upper layer—again sealing under ends.

Return to the portion of dough that has been set aside. Repeat shaping the Houska to make the second bread. Let rise until double. Bake at 350° for 50 minutes. Cool. Store in a cool place or freeze several weeks to blend flavors. Slice. Toast. Butter. Enjoy.

VISITING

Lidmilla and Johan Prokopec with Albina (our Grandma Deml),
Ludmilla and Mary

Our parents not only took us to our own church, they took
us to visit other churches and cemeteries that were important
to our families. One of these was the tiny Catholic church
Mom attended as a child.

In the farming community of Saco, a little wooden church
was built across the road from Mom's country schoolhouse—
and was just about the same size. The schoolhouse was
where early settlers had worshipped before the church was
built in 1876. The land for the church was donated by a
zealous, community-minded Catholic Czech named Vaclav
Pavek. The church was named St. Vaclav in honor of both
this man himself as well as for his namesake: the Czech's
beloved St. Vaclav—the patron saint of Bohemia, the
homeland of our people—who is known to most of us today
as St. Wenceslaus. The church in Saco was identified as St.
Wenceslaus Mission Church.

When we visited the church, known to us as Saco Church,

the seating was still as it had been in Mom's childhood. The men sat on one side and the women on the other side of the aisle—perhaps to help keep everyone's attention focused primarily on God.

St. Wenceslaus Church stood about a mile from Mom's childhood home, seven miles southwest of Owatonna, in one of the first Czech settlements in Steele County. The area was known as Saco then, but was originally called Moravia, after Frank Moravia, its first settler, who lived there in 1860.

In 1962, this historic wood-framed church, St. Wenceslaus Church, was moved onto the grounds of the Steele County Historical Society located on the Steele County Fair Grounds.

As a child, Carol was unaware of a cemetery near Mom's birthplace and the Saco Church. However, years later she and Mom attended a Memorial Day Mass at Saco Cemetery. Saco Church had already been moved onto the Steele County Fair Grounds by that time. Numerous Catholic folk congregated to remember their beloved friends and relatives buried at this site.

There are many cemeteries in Steele County. Holy Trinity Cemetery is located about a half mile from Holy Trinity Church located in Litomysl, Minnesota. Holy Trinity Church is the country church Dad attended as a child. We liked to go there for its annual summer festival. Picnic tables were scattered on the lawn with the wide-open spaces and— farmland—all around the Church premises. A big noon meal was followed by time for the farmers and their wives (and for visiting grown children and grandchildren) to share family stories and for the kids to play games.

Years later, friends and family formed a procession to follow a wagon pulled by horses carrying the body of Uncle Edward's grandson (Larry) to be buried in the Litomysl cemetery a half-mile down the gravel road from Holy Trinity Church.

Holy Trinity Church was so different from our family's church, which was right in the middle of the town of Owatonna. Mom and Dad were long-time members of Sacred

Heart Church in the city of Owatonna. They are buried in Sacred Heart Cemetery on the south edge of Owatonna on what used to be Highway 65 (now County Road 45).

As children, we visited these cemeteries to remember our relatives and to pray for them at their grave sites. These childhood visits to the cemeteries often occurred on Memorial Day weekend. We placed flowers on the gravesites. While at the cemetery, visitors and families gathered to share memories of family history.

Cemetery visits were the most important way of doing genealogic work before the computer-based data searches of today. The visits prompted our parents to tell us stories about the people buried there. Dad told us the sad story of his grandfather's death, a suicide, because Dad was a great believer in teaching us about death as well as life. He didn't shy away from talking about such things as illness, death, divorce, and unfortunate events.

Dad couldn't have hidden the suicide event if he'd wanted to: Everyone knew about it. In those days, newspapers would print all the grim, graphic details about a suicide. The newspaper carried the graphic details of his grandfather's death, as was typical of newspapers of 1917. Following is the article written about our great-grandpa.

The body of John Prokopec, the aged farmer whose disappearance was told of in last week's Journal-Chronicle, was found last Saturday morning in a small place of timber about a mile and a half from the home of his son, Frank Prokopec, in Blooming Prairie Township, with whom he had been living. The old gentleman had been missing for four days, and had left behind him a note stating that he would never be seen again. From the time he was missed on the preceding Tuesday evening, until the finding of the body, searching parties had been out looking for him.

The manner of his death was evident. He had blown off the top of his head with a shotgun by means of a string tied to the trigger and a tree.

His grave lies outside the cemetery confines because the man took his own life. Since the death of his wife, the seventy-five-year-old man had been in failing health and suffered with depression.

> **CAROL:** *In our childhood family reminiscences (now called oral tradition), visits to cemeteries were a focal point of genealogical searching. Today, I enjoy the cemetery runs throughout Steele County which were originated by a group of our male cousins. After much cajoling from me as a female cousin, the guys finally relented and invited me and other female cousins to join them in learning more about our relatives and "celebrating" their lives. Celebrating included tipping a glass of wine with laughter at some of the funny stories the "guys" remembered about our ancestors. The "run" helped me get to know my living cousins better. Also, the shared stories filled in missing gaps about those who died.*

Our great-grandfather, Johan Prokopec, was born in Dolni Dobrouce, Bohemia, in the mid-1800s. In the spring of 1893, he, his wife and children had their trunks filled with belongings and boarded a ship for the United States of America. They settled in Steele County in Summit Township and found land to farm in the Bohemian community of Litomysl. After purchasing land in section 10, they built a log cabin the same year and began clearing the land. He and his family were active members of Holy Trinity Church.

> **CAROL:** *I had never been to the Bohemian Slovanian Burial Ground in Summit Township where our great-grandpa was buried. So my cousins included this cemetery in the run. There his grave was, all alone, on the outskirts of the fenced-in cemetery. A great feeling of sadness enveloped me. His gravesite was not included with those "inside" the fence.*

So Dad didn't hide the sad facts of his grandfather's death. Johan (John) Prokopec was not buried in a Catholic

144

Cemetery but outside the fence of the Bohemian Slovanian Burial Ground in Summit Township. Although our great-grandfather had been a staunch Catholic during his life, he had taken his own life—thus committing what the church considered a mortal sin and costing him the privilege of being laid to rest in holy ground.

The practice of the Catholic Church as well as obituary coverage in newspapers has changed. It is no longer church doctrine that people who commit suicide must be banished for their despair and weakness by being excluded from the consecrated grounds of church cemeteries. Even those long dead, like our great-grandfather, can now be moved to holy ground upon the church's approval of a family member's request. Perhaps someday great-grandpa may be moved inside to a site near his wife's grave.

Over the years, Sacred Heart Church supplied pastors to both Holy Trinity and St. Wenceslaus Churches. To this date, the country church at Litomysl remains active with a small parish Catholic School. However, due to the shortage of priests, the church has made changes. With the addition of Masses being held on Saturday to accommodate the Sunday liturgy, the pastor of Sacred Heart Church covers liturgies and other sacramental needs of the Litomysl Church, just as they served the Saco Church in the early 1900s.

Mom and Dad enjoyed taking us to visit their brothers and sisters. For us, it was an opportunity to get to know uncles and aunts as well as cousins and new environments. Not all of our uncles and aunts were farmers. Some owned grocery stores, managed their rental properties, or piloted planes—all new adventures for farm girls. We drove to far away places (it seemed they were far away to small girls). Places like Mankato, Eagle Lake, New Richland, Ellendale, Hope, Waldorf, and, of course, Owatonna were all within a forty-mile radius of our home. Although most of these places were in our very own Steele County or in a nearby county, these visits expanded our horizons to people with different attitudes about life, adventure, and travel.

For instance, Uncle Eddie Wesely owned a grocery store in Hope. There were the usual grocery items available: candy, fresh scooped ice cream, and fresh garden produce. But the wonder of wonders was the fresh cut beef available. Dad was astounded by Uncle Eddie's strength. He could lift a beef half all by himself and then cut just a steak or the ribs ordered.

> **CAROL:** *We went upstairs from the grocery store to their home for a brief visit. Our cousin David was older than us girls. While we munched on cookies and lemonade served by Aunt Luella, David entertained us. He played ragtime, jazz or classical selections on the piano.*

The idea of having one's home above one's business was a novel idea, but not uncommon in those days. Uncle Joseph owned a grocery store in Waldorf. He and his wife somehow managed to raise five children in their tiny upstairs apartment. His wife, Ag, wrote wonderful columns for the Owatonna Daily People's Press.

Uncle Tom was a commercial airline pilot. Although we never flew with him in that capacity, we did fly over our area in a small plane. When we had the opportunity to have a picture taken of our farm, Dad made arrangements with the pilot to give us girls a ride over our farm.

> **Carol:** *Flying was a new experience for me. We flew from the Owatonna airport over our farm and surrounding areas. The pilot tipped the plane from left to right so that we could get a view of buildings and the acreage surrounding it. We flew over Dan Gainey's farm and saw the magnificent Arabian horses running in the massive white-fenced corrals. Arabian horses were extremely expensive; therefore, they were rare in our area.*
>
> *In 1969, Uncle Tom flew a small plane to return me home for our farm's auction sale.*

Once when the family was visiting our Wesely grandparents, Carol walked the few blocks from their house to downtown to window shop. After a while, she walked back towards home, whistling as she walked on the street opposite the courthouse. At that point, a car drove alongside her, driving very slowly to keep pace with her. A man rolled down his window and began talking to her. Carol stiffened and walked faster, but he stayed by her. The man tried to get her to get into the car with him, but she knew better than to do that. After what seemed like forever, the man drove on.

SCHOOL DAYS

From being sheltered children, we expanded our vision once we began attending District #22—a one-room country elementary school. Our school was located one-half mile north on the highway, then one-half mile west on a gravel road. The school bordered one of the square-mile farming sections of Steele County, Minnesota. Rose, Carol, and Cathy spent eight years in country school, while Lori attended only two years before the country school closed.

About eighteen children in grades one through eight attended the little school. During Rose's first year in school, Mark, the eighth-grade neighbor boy, stopped by our house at exactly 8:10 a.m. to walk Rose to school. By the time Rose was in second grade, her eighth-grade neighbor had moved on to high school and Rose was left to walk to school each day on her own.

> **ROSE:** *I was a very cautious second-grade girl. Walking to school one cool crisp spring morning, I was dressed in a jumper and sweater, wearing long brown cotton stockings and brand new pull-on rubber boots. With a scarf around my neck and a lunch bucket in hand, I walked quickly.*
>
> *Ordinarily, I walked around the square mile, first on*

148

the highway and then turned onto the gravel road. As I hurried along, I could see children in the school yard playing games. Spring was coming, snow was melting, and I wanted to join in the games before the school bell rang. But that day I was so eager to join them that I took a short cut, cutting diagonally across the field. I cut across the rich black soil of the plowed field and scooted over and under two barbed-wire fences. The shortcut was not a good idea: Minnesota black soil often freezes to a depth of eight to twelve inches. When spring comes (very slowly) even if the snow has disappeared, the thawing soil is slick and slippery. As I walked further and further across the field, my boots became more and more coated with mud. The suction of boots trying to release from the mud frightened me. I stopped dead still.

After a moment of pausing, I attempted to take another step only to feel my foot lifting, not out of the mud, but out of the boot. That occurred easily because coats, shoes, and boots were purchased one or two sizes larger to allow for growth. I stopped again. I would not step out of these new boots and leave them in the field.

I could see the school children gather at the fence to watch me wondering why I was standing motionless in the field. Noticing the unusual gathering of children at the school, a neighbor across the road realized that I was standing still in the field. After watching several moments and seeing no movement on my part, she phoned my parents to say, "Rose seems to be in the field stuck in the mud."

Dad immediately began to plan a rescue. He considered bringing the tractor, but it might also get stuck in the mud. He no longer had horses; and there were two fences to cross. What to do? And then calmer

149

thoughts: He could walk across the field. He drove as close as he could to the area in the field, parked the truck, climbed the fence and strode into the field. With joy and trepidation, I watched him coming. After all, I was walking to school. I was not supposed to be cutting across the neighbor's field.

He picked me up, hung me—a very muddy bundle— over his arm, reached down for the one boot still stuck in the mud and carried me out of the field to the truck. I needed a hot bath and clean clothes. I suspect I did not attend school that day.

At school, two of the older students were assigned the weekly task of carrying drinking water from the neighbor's farm to the school. They carried two tall cylindrical water buckets with covers to the school. They poured the water into a water fountain located in the cloak room. Here students could get a drink from a dipper shared by all. We had to ask permission to go into the cloak room to get a drink of water, but we were usually asked to wait until recess. Some things just never change.

It was a privilege to be released from some classroom time. And it was an honor to be assigned some of the regular classroom duties. But, if we were assigned to sweep the tiny outhouse at the back of the school yard, it was considered more of a punishment.

ROSE: *If I finished my assignments early, I would earn the privilege of a visit to the library, a very small room located behind our desks. There I could read and choose books to take home. The Bobbsey Twins series was my favorite. I soon read all the books in that small library several times, but it was special just to sit quietly alone in that space.*

Older students were given the privilege of raising the American flag on the outside pole before classes began each morning. Then, the person who raised the flag rang the large school bell that hung in the outer porch. The students inside the school stood, faced the flag, and recited the Pledge of Allegiance before classes began. Years later, the words "under God" were inserted into the pledge, to say "one nation, under God."

One teacher taught all subjects for all eight grades. Therefore, older students were encouraged to help the teacher and younger students. Students were assigned a desk with little ones near the front, near the teacher and near the windows. Assignments for the day and questions for different grades and subjects were written on the blackboard. For this reason, the upper grade students were seated near the blackboards.

There was a pattern or schedule to each day and week. Each class was allotted a ten-to-fifteen minute session with the teacher. For example, the teacher would call the fifth grade to come to the front of the room and be seated at a small table. All the other students could hear the teacher and the class at the front discussing their lesson. This gave a first-grader an opportunity to hear similar material repeated eight times by the time they completed eighth grade.

Depending on the subject, students might be asked to read aloud, discuss the material, answer questions, draw diagrams on the blackboard, work arithmetic problems at the board, or to go up to the wall map to locate historical or geographical places in the world.

Students kept busy while at school preparing for each class. There was time to do assignments at school and students could ask each other to help solve a problem or answer a written question.

ROSE: *I loved school and quickly completed my assignments. I never recall homework from grade school. However, starting in the ninth grade, I was given hours of homework.*

151

Everyone brought a noon lunch. A few students carried a small thermos of milk or hot cocoa (if lucky), or hot soup in their dinner buckets, or lunch pails, as they were called.

At the end of the school day, everyone was eager to go home. A little student would pick up the chalkboard erasers and go outside to dust erasers—clap them together in the breeze and watch the chalk dust blow away. An upper class student went outside to pull down the flag, fold it, and bring it inside. This student was first to be excused. Meanwhile, others were excused grade by grade to gather coats, boots, lunch buckets, and papers to carry home. Each grade then returned to their seats, and finally, row by row, the students were excused to go home.

Rarely did anyone have a ride home from school—we walked. At the end of the school driveway, eight or nine kids turned either east or west to walk home on the gravel road.

ROSE: *It is interesting to note that there were about an equal number of boys and girls departing in either direction. As a young girl, I remember the older boys running and pushing and teasing as we walked home. Fortunately, the older neighbor boy was always there ready to protect me. At the corner, we again parted with some turning north and some turning south on the highway.*

Our school routine changed on Friday, which was cleaning day. Blackboards were washed and floors swept clean. Just before the noon lunch break, a younger student was asked to walk around with a small basket to collect waste paper and then empty the basket.

By Friday afternoon, the country kids were eager for the weekend to begin. The teacher used this time for art or music classes for the whole student body. If the weather was fine and the students had had a busy and productive week in the classroom, the teacher extended the afternoon recess and all played games together. Compare that to a physical education class today!

"Anti-over" was a favorite game at school for recess time. We threw a softball or smaller rubber ball over a building, yelling "anti-anti-over" and then raced around trying to tag someone from the team on the other side who was trying to catch the ball. We played this game at home, too. Our two-story house was too high for us girls to make the ball fly up and over. So we threw it over the granary, and we did not have to worry about windows.

Of course, injuries occur while playing. Rose suffered several. She loved to play games, especially softball, but her eagerness resulted in a few injuries and—to be sure—great concern on the part of our parents. Eighteen students, ages six to fourteen, played work-up. This meant each had a turn to bat, regardless of how many outs or runs in the game. In first grade, Rose could barely wait a turn to bat, so she stepped too close to the batter before her. He struck the ball and let the bat swing out of his hands. It hit her forehead above her right eye. That was one puffy black eye for a few days.

On another occasion, she did hit the ball and ran as hard as she could sliding into first base, and fractured her collarbone. Did she score a run that day?

A Mother's Day program was scheduled when Carol was about twelve years old. All the mothers were seated awaiting the performance of the poems, skits, and songs the children had practiced over the past weeks. Carol sang the "Our Father." Not only was the audience delighted, but she took great pleasure in having shared her vocal talent.

Spelling bees were a given when Rose was in her later years at country school. She was our family's star speller. Dad would coach her sitting at our oak table. In front of him lay a newspaper filled with lists of words for the contest. Rose listened to the word Dad pronounced, spoke the word once, spelled it, and finally repeated the word. Rose won the school contest three times, each time qualifying her for the county spelling bee. Unfortunately, each year, shortly before the contest, she came down with tonsillitis. Still, she always recuperated enough to participate, and one year she took second place. The family was sure she would have won if only she had not been ill.

> **ROSE:** *Never to be forgotten or misspelled is the word I missed: commissioned. I spelled it c o m m o s s i o n e d instead of commissioned.*

Not only did we study at the dining room table, but also we played board games, especially long games of Monopoly because the game could remain set up while we ate meals at the kitchen table. That was also where we put together thousand-piece jigsaw puzzles with Mom—sometimes into the wee hours of the morning.

> **ROSE:** *Once during high school, I was assigned a project that required me to list my hobbies, followed by a suggestion of a possible career path based on each one. Back then, as to this day, I enjoyed jigsaw puzzles with Mom on those dark, cold winter nights in Minnesota. Perplexed, I asked the counselor what working puzzles would bring to a career. His answer was quick and exactly what I have needed for the achievements in my lifetime, "Your persistence and patience will be your life-long approach to any challenge you face." I think he was right.*

Our parents always stressed the importance of education, even for girls, which was not common at that time. It was doubly unusual in their case because neither one of them completed high school. This wasn't because of any dislike of school. They'd been withdrawn from school by their parents to help their families, which was not an unusual reason for children in any family in those days.

One of Mom's favorite teachers was a demanding, tiny young woman. She insisted that the children speak correct English both in the classroom and in the school yard.

(Students came from homes where Czech, German, and English were spoken.) In the small one-room classroom, it was just this little teacher facing her students who ranged in age from six to sixteen, some standing taller than she. Insisting on English as a common language, she maintained strict discipline.

Mom and Dad loved to read books and newspapers. Mom read about and enrolled in a home health/first-aid class. Subsequently, she taught Carol a bit of what she had learned.

> **CAROL:** *When I was a young girl, Mom took a home health/first aid class. How to make a bed with hospital-tight square corners was one of the tricks she passed on to me. At that time, there were no fitted sheets. We secured sheets by tucking a large portion at the foot of the bed beneath the mattress; another large portion was secured at the top of the bed beneath the mattress. Next, at each corner the sheet was pulled straight out and up at the sides to form a triangle. Then, the bottom portion of the triangle was tucked beneath the mattress to make a square corner. The sheet was so tight and smooth that a penny could bounce if dropped on it. Mom never made us drop a coin on it to check for tightness.*

Carol found that reading the wrong material caught Mom's attention.

> **CAROL:** *We were expected to nap in our beds, something I, as a teenager, didn't think I needed. So, rather than napping, I read. Mom discovered that I purchased and read trashy magazines—as she thought of them. She banned them. It put a damper on my reading pleasure.*

Mom loved books and she read to us as well as encouraged us to read. *The Birds' Christmas Carol*, by Kate Douglas Wiggin, touched Mom's heart... and thus Carol received her name.

ROSE: *That very book, The Birds' Christmas Carol, is such a favorite of mine that I later collected original copies of it to give my children. Its story has a lot in common with my family of nine children.*

Each Christmas season, Mom read to us the special newspaper serial.

CAROL: *Prior to Christmas each year, the Daily People's Press published a chapter-a-day children's Christmas story. Each day I anticipated hearing Mom read the next chapter.*

Mom took us to the Owatonna Public Library regularly. It was an imposing stone structure. The children's books were housed in the basement where we selected books to take home. Even today, one of the places Carol frequents is the local library.

When we were growing up, Mom demanded perfect pronunciation and complete sentences. When we misspoke, she promptly corrected us. Although she had only a seventh grade education, she was a great speller and spoke very correct English.

CAROL: *Mom was a great listener. When I tried to ask her a question that was quite clear in my mind but confusing to her, she would say, "Carol, start at the beginning."*

Mom's English expertise qualified her to work at the newspaper. Mom enjoyed her work for the newspaper editor but disliked the editor's dirty habit of spitting into his spittoon, which he often missed creating a sticky, icky mess.

During the first two weeks of summer vacation, Franciscan Sisters came to Owatonna to teach country students who were unable to attend the year-round classes at St. Mary's Grade School — right next door to Sacred Heart Church.

156

The two-weeks of "vacation school" or "Sister School" as we called it that took place immediately after elementary school was over, was a wonderful experience for a country girl. We were asked to sacrifice pennies or nickels for the missionaries in China and Africa. Each day that we contributed we would receive a beautiful holy card with a prayer and picture of a saint.

ROSE: *I was fascinated by the idea of teaching or doing missionary work in Africa. I loved to play school and teach my younger sisters and cousins. I dreamed that someday I would teach first grade in Africa. Sixty years later, Dick and I visited a small village in central Kenya. The village was surrounded by a twelve-foot high wall of interwoven heavily-spined branches and limbs to keep out lions and other predators. Ten beehive-like low huts provided some privacy to each family. In the center of the compound was the fire pit for cooking. It was surrounded by a wide path.*

When tourists arrived, the women and children spread their hand-made jewelry and trinkets on blankets in the pathway. The tourists entered one of the larger huts in the village. Each hut—constructed of mud and cattle dung—was built by the bride-to-be, a required dowry.

Outside the village compound, under a tree, was a small wooden school house—much smaller than our one-room schools in Minnesota. It had room for a small bleacher. About two dozen young children sat on the bleacher facing a desk and single slate blackboard. The children were reciting the alphabet and counting in a singsong style as they learned English. For that one moment in the classroom, I wanted to stay and teach those delightful small children. Of course, that was not possible. I was a visitor from America.

As I stepped out of this small dark room into the bright sunlight of the African day, I could see a tall herdsman with a staff returning from the fields. Looking up into the vast expanse above and beyond the village, there appeared a wondrous triple rainbow in the sky behind him. What a nice way to end my dream of teaching in Africa.

During recess at Sister School, we played most games outside. Both girls enjoyed playing Jacks—either outside or indoors.

CAROL: *We played with a hard rubber bouncing ball and ten metal jacks. I learned this game during "Sister School" recess—playing on the sidewalk near Sacred Heart Catholic Church. But later, I enjoyed playing Jacks with my cousins. Indoors, I could sit on the floor for hours at a time—legs bent behind me.*

In the game of Jacks, we played many different routines: Babies, Baskets, Upcast, Downcast, Half Cast, Whole Cast, Quarter Cast, Snake in the Garden, Scratch the Match, Butter in the Cup, Baby in the High Chair, Pig in the Pen, Pig under the Pen, Pig over the Pen, Half Moon, Whole Moon, All Around the World, and Mummies. In order to get to Mummies, we first had to complete each routine: onesies, twosies, and so forth through tens. If a person missed the ball or moved a jack in any part of a routine, the opponent took her turn because not catching the ball or moving a jack was a blunder.

Carol found Mummies the most difficult routine. All ten parts had to be completed without touching a superfluous jack or missing the ball. Finally, triumph. Hurrah.

Activities outside of class also occupied our grade-school years.

ROSE: *I was given the opportunity to take piano lessons from the Franciscan nuns who taught in St. Mary's Catholic School in Owatonna. One-half hour of practice was required each day. My teacher was very*

158

particular about posture, poise of the arm and hands that curved over the keys. Each piece was counted out-loud to the time specified. We did not purchase a metronome to strike the time.

Sister stressed that correct fingering was important when learning classical selections. The nun's hand curved above my hand while I played. If I struck a wrong note, her finger struck down on the finger I should have used. Ouch.

How exciting to prepare for the recital. I remember shopping for a navy taffeta dress that swished as I walked to the piano. Although very nervous that I might forget some of the notes, I felt grown-up, pretty, and confident.

Each student memorized a song to play at the spring recital. It was a big event for a small audience. Recitals were usually held in the convent's piano room where guests could overflow into the adjoining hall where we took piano lessons. Rose played in three recitals and played one duet with Carol. Mom helped us as we practiced for the big day. When Carol was old enough to take lessons, money ran short.

CAROL: *One day I was in town with Dad. Walking slightly behind him with eyes downcast, I picked up a roll of bills, "Dad, look what I found." Upon examining it, he commented, "$20 in $1 bills."*

Receiving no response after advertising in the newspaper, Dad said, "Carol, you can use that $20 for piano lessons." Piano lessons from the Franciscan Sisters in town cost a dollar an hour. Sometimes, after supper, I practiced piano in order to get out of wiping dishes.

Piano lessons provided another special time for Rose.

ROSE: *After my lesson I walked three blocks to the home of Grandma and Grandpa Wesely. I walked past a tiny grocery store, wishing I had money for candy or ice cream. Luckily, a treat was waiting at Grandma's house. She always had a jar filled with homemade cookies. Grandma Wesely served me Hermits (very soft, spicy, date and nut goodies).*

Hermits:

Cream 1 c. brown sugar, ½ c. white sugar and ½ c. butter. Add 3 eggs; cream well.

Mix together ½ tsp. cinnamon, ¼ tsp. cloves, ¼ tsp. salt and 1 C. flour.

Raisin mixture: Boil 2 T. water and 1 tsp. salt with ¾ C. finely-chopped raisins and ¾ C. finely-chopped walnuts. Simmer until raisins are soft.

Alternate adding dry ingredients and raisin mixture to cream mixture.

Drop rounded teaspoonfuls of batter 2 inches apart on lightly greased baking sheet. Bake at 375° about 10 minutes.

ROSE: *Dad did not mind waiting for me during my piano lesson. He and Grandpa spent the time playing pinochle, and were also served a treat which only they loved—a SMELLY treat—Braunschweiger with crackers and Limburger cheese—with one of Grandma's home-canned cucumber pickles.*

160

HIGH SCHOOL AND BEYOND

Rose worked hard on her piano lessons and later tried to play the cello in high school. The conductor asked her to join the orchestra. A cello player was needed to round out the program. The high school music department loaned her a cello.

ROSE: *Although I had three private lessons with the conductor, he soon realized I was tone deaf and unable to tune my instrument. My orchestra career lasted less than two weeks. I never had a chance to even join the orchestra in practice. There is a tuning instrument now available to those who cannot hear the notes. I recall loving the feel of drawing the bow across the strings to create the soft tone on a cello and to this day enjoy the sound of a cello. Although I cannot play, I can listen.*

Carol found an interest in sewing. Through 4-H and home economics class, she learned the basics of color, style, and using a sewing machine. High school sewing classes opened new horizons for her—a direction she had never anticipated. Now she could choose what she wanted to wear from a variety of patterns in a catalog or from the dime store selection.

Mom helped Carol choose the fabric. One project Carol was especially proud of was a dress made of a beautiful soft orange and brown floral cotton fabric. The dress was a two-piece affair: The blouse had a short-sleeved scooped neckline and the full skirt was gathered. She displayed it as a 4-H project for the fair and won a ribbon and a prize. Unfortunately, she later realized that the color didn't suit her complexion. Even though disappointed, she wore the dress to high school until she outgrew it.

Later, Mom helped Carol sew a teal, pale green, and violet floral dress for a special dance at school. Wearing the dress with its poofed-out bottom edge gathered upwards from its underside lining, she felt elegant and pretty. Mom also shopped with Carol for clothing. A fitted yellow A-line dress was a favorite because of its swirling skirt. The color and style made heads turn and compliments abound. In this dress, Carol got compliments whenever she wore it.

One black skirt that Carol did not make but insisted on wearing to school drew dark looks of displeasure from Mom because it didn't hang—it clung. This black skirt showed every little curve Carol possessed in a day and age when disapproval of such clothing was evident. Feeling guilty, Carol only wore it a few times.

> **CAROL:** *In retrospect, my sewing classes and the lure of the sewing machine influenced my later years when quilting became a creative outlet for me. However, after twenty-five years of quilting, I still have trouble with color selection. Fortunately, I have a husband and sons who have an eye for color and placement of design. Why not take advantage of their abilities? So, I often ask their assistance.*

Carol also used her skills with the English language to begin writing.

> **CAROL:** *As a freshman, I wrote my first book in pencil, printing each and every letter. (I wonder if that was a part of the assignment.) The class project helped*

me put into words my past history—short as it was—as well as my future plans. I thought I might like to be a secretary, so as a part of the project, I interviewed Cousin Jinny who had a secretarial position.

After completing a typing class during my sophomore year, I asked for a typewriter. I was thrilled to receive an Olivetti typewriter for my sixteenth birthday. Use of my typing skills did not materialize immediately. However, my dream came true much later. I held secretarial positions for nearly twenty years before retirement.

Carol and Dad

Like Mom, Rose wanted to become a teacher. She did eventually teach school, but her path there took an unexpected turn. In high school, she chose academic classes that would prepare her to go to college. She hoped to attend either St. Catherine's College or St. Mary's College to major in elementary education.

ROSE: *Always practical, I chose home economics for my one elective class during my senior year in high school. By chance, the home economics teacher walked*

163

*past the desk in the principal's office and noticed some
application forms in his wastebasket. She retrieved the
forms for the first annual Betty Crocker Homemaker
of Tomorrow competition and asked me to take the
written exam the following day.*

*The search began with a multiple choice test followed
by a written essay. Among those taking the test, I won
the school award and then the State Award: a $1,500
scholarship to the school of my choice. Continuous
observation and interviews by the judges, who joined
us for the week-long trip, were used to select the winner
of a $5,000 scholarship.*

*A national winner would be chosen from forty-eight
contestants. It was almost like a Miss America contest.
Imagine, choosing only one person from all forty-eight
states. The year, 1955, was before Alaska and Hawaii
were named to statehood.*

*I needed clothes for my week-long trip east. A rose-
colored sundress and jacket caught my eye but did not
fit my budget. My aunt Mary was an accomplished
seamstress, as was her mother, Rose Wesely. We
brought the dress, with several others, home on
approval. Aunt Mary looked closely at the dress and
said, "This looks simple." She carefully laid it out on
the floor to observe the lines of the dress and designed
a similar pattern. We purchased fabric and she made
a beautiful sundress and jacket for me, just for this trip.*

*I was to appear on national television as the Minnesota
Betty Crocker Homemaker of Tomorrow, along with
the winners from all the other states. What a thrill
it was to have Eddie Fisher at the televised banquet!
Other luminaries present were our evening's speaker,
the Secretary of the Treasury, and Debbie Reynolds—
newly engaged to Eddie Fisher. This event closed our*

week's trip and the highlight—naming of the national winner.

Of course, Dad had to have television to watch this program, so he rented a television for one month during my senior year. The radio and the Owatonna Daily People's Press—not a television—were our sources of local and world news.

Alabama's Homemaker of Tomorrow was awarded the national $5,000 scholarship.

With the $1,500 scholarship, Rose still had to consider a choice of a major in a college she could afford. The Catholic college cost was more than our family could afford even with the scholarship. (Remember that she paid less than $1,000 total for her first year at the University of Minnesota.) By the end of her senior year of high school, she had completed ten years in 4-H and worked at the county and state fairs. She had developed a great interest in home economics. At a much lower cost, she found she could attend the University of Minnesota and major in home economics education rather than pursue her first dream of elementary education at a private Catholic college.

Rose kept a small expense book the first year of college. The sum total of all that she spent that year including postage stamps, gum, candy bars, bus rides, food, dorm expenses, movies, and textbooks was $993. In addition to the $1500 scholarship, her 4-H baby beef sold at auction for $401. On campus, Rose found work in the library where she worked for her entire college career. The second year of college she became a member of the 4-H sorority, Clovia. The third year she applied for a position as house manager of Clovia. In exchange, she received room and board for being the house manager. One evening a week for the last three years in college Rose prepared the evening meal for a fraternity and last, but not least, earned a final $50 scholarship her last quarter at the University of Minnesota.

165

Because of her ten years in 4-H, work at the county extension office two summers before college, plus courses in food preparation and clothing her freshman year in college, Rose applied for and accepted work as a summer 4-H agent. Providentially, Rose was hired as a summer 4-H agent after her freshman year because it was crucial to have courses in food preparation and clothing prior to being hired. This was uncommon because most students took those courses their sophomore year and were not eligible to be hired. She worked four summers as a 4-H agent and earned hours toward social security. After all of the part-time work, summer employment, the scholarships and careful budgeting, Rose graduated debt-free.

In addition to her college studies, Rose attended daily Mass at the Newman Center on campus each year. She volunteered with the youth group at church (above the Newman Center) for a year. She was on the campus student council for three years and served as secretary for the council one year. As a college senior, she was president of the Phi Upsilon Omicron honorary home economics sorority.

Rose began to sew in her high school home economics elective course. Although not expert on the treadle machine (she had trouble keeping her feet rocking in the correct rhythm needed for a neat row of stitches), she persisted in stitching away. The jerky motions often broke the thread, which meant that the machine would have to be re-threaded (an irksome interruption). The skipped stitches in a seam line also posed a problem because clothing was likely to tear at those points.

Ever practical, Rose made her first big purchase after graduating from college: a sewing machine. She sold her car for $100 and purchased a portable, electric, featherweight Singer sewing machine for exactly $100. It was a gem. Even today that model is considered one of the most reliable electric sewing machines ever made. Her daughter still uses it today.

Dad was pleased that Rose had graduated from college and wanted her to teach at least one year before getting married. He feared that her years of education would be wasted. But Rose had other plans—to marry the man she met at the Newman Center at a Catholic youth meeting.

> **ROSE:** *When I told Dad of my plans to marry in the fall after my June graduation, he suggested that I not waste my college education. Would I consider at least one year of teaching before marriage? Dad wanted me to experience all I could in my life and to use my home economics education in the years ahead. I did not agree with Dad and made plans to marry that fall. Neither Dad, nor I, would have imagined how much I would use my home economics degree in raising nine children and creating a home in fourteen different houses.*

Mother, Rose, Rose's friend Betty, Cathy, and Carol went to Nicollet Mall in Minneapolis to shop. We were looking for Rose's wedding dress as well as for dresses for Carol, the maid-of-honor, and the other two bridesmaids. Trying on the dresses was exhilarating: how beautiful the subtle champagne-colored dresses styled like the dresses worn by singers on the Lawrence Welk show.

Carol recalls that shopping for the wedding meant a fascinating day in the big city of Minneapolis. We ate lunch at LeAnn Chin's Chinese restaurant. The hanging Chinese lanterns, the deep red wallpaper, and the carpeted staircase were lovely. We ate on the second level. The exotic taste of the food opened up a new world from that experienced on the farm.

Rose's wedding reception was to be held in our home. Before carpet could be installed, we had to paint and redecorate.

Mom not only had a good eye for style and color in clothing, but also had good taste in house decorating. Although she didn't have the money for major changes in the house décor, she did have some painting done. The biggest project was the time she had the living room and kitchen painted. Both needed freshening. They were discolored from the wood oils and coal dust of the furnace.

ROSE: *The painter arrived with several cans of white paint. He set to work coloring it with drops of color he brought along. The painter mixed paint on the spot in our home. Mom had no paint chips or color formulas to give him: They didn't exist yet. So the painter kept stirring and stirring and adjusting and adjusting, trying to create the colors Mom had in her mind: a creamy white to lighten the kitchen (which had a brown-stain, varnished slat ceiling), and robin's-egg blue for the front room. It took a while for the man to get the colors right. Mom knew exactly what she wanted and insisted that the painter work until the color exactly matched what she imagined.*

Of course, the living room must have major redecorating before the wedding guests arrive. A horsehair sofa and a patterned wool area carpet from the first years of Mom and Dad's marriage were replaced. New drapes were hung and beautiful light beige wall-to-wall carpet was installed. How elegant everything looked!

But it all changed three days before the wedding. Rose and Dick were babysitting Lori, age two and one-half, when they suddenly realized that the house was quiet—way too quiet for a toddler, Rose jumped up to look for Lori. Oh no. Panic. Shock. Dismay. What is Lori doing?

ROSE: *I found her in the corner of the living room, drawing with a tube of bright red lipstick. She was drawing on the light-colored, brand new carpet! "No, No!" We panicked wondering what we could do to remove the lipstick before Mom returned. We made many phone calls to find out how to remove the lipstick markings. But we found simple soap and water was all we had. We rubbed and scrubbed until most of the color at least lightened. Then we pulled the chair over to cover the spot. I don't know if Mom ever knew about this almost-debacle.*

168

Dick and Rose were married in the fall following their graduation from the University of Minnesota. They moved seven times in the first four years of marriage, causing Uncle Ed, Rose's godfather, great concern. Uncle Ed told Dad, "I'm worried about Rose. She keeps having babies and moves all the time. Her husband can't hold a job and, to make matters worse, they drive an old car."

Four generations: Edward, Jim, Joseph and Marie Deml

Dad quickly assured Edward that these moves were based on promotions. Dad also laughed about the comment on the old car, knowing that new cars were a status symbol in this farming community. Meanwhile, Dad admired her husband's thriftiness and his ability to maintain and service his own car.

ROSE: *I was fortunate to be a stay-at-home Mom. We had lived in Wisconsin ten years when I was asked to teach home economics a half day. Once again Dick was transferred—this time to West Virginia—and I began substitute teaching there and was able to work the same hours as the hours our children attended school. That gave me the advantage of working and being at home*

169

with our family after school. As a substitute teacher in all areas, I soon learned I preferred teaching math over home economics and also could see that there would never be an opening in the home economics department. Meanwhile, there was always a demand for math teachers.

With a degree in education and practice teaching completed, I needed only a few credits to become a math teacher. During six years of substitute teaching in many subject areas, I renewed my love of math from high school days. In 1955, girls were still expected to become teachers or nurses and not pursue mathematics.

I took advantage of classes in late afternoon and summer classes in math. The day I completed my math degree, I accepted a full-time math position and taught eighth grade math and algebra for seventeen years. During that time there was never an opening in home economics.

During her high school years, Rose was the studious one in our family. Carol was more interested in people, especially people of the opposite sex. They were the highlight of her high school years. She had her first date when she was a freshman. Although she was interested in boys, she was shy around them but good at flirting. Having no brothers, she was sometimes inept in knowing just how to deal with situations that involved boys.

CAROL: *Phil asked me to the homecoming game and dance. Students who lived in town had learned to dance in elementary school, but not in country school. I had no experience with dancing. Scared about making a mistake and a fool of myself on the dance floor, I asked him to dance only in the darkened corner of the gym. He humored me, but never invited me out again.*

During Carol's sophomore year, she dated a tall, dark-haired, gentle senior, who owned a motorcycle. Riding on

Francis' motorcycle with arms around his waist and the wind blowing through her hair was exciting. The year went all too quickly.

In the spring of her junior year, a new friendship came her way. Polio, a dread disease of the 1940s and 50s hit Tom's family with a vengeance. Tom's twin brother, Ted, escaped major life changes. Tom's older brother died at age 13. The day after his funeral, Tom was stricken, remained in an iron lung for a couple of weeks, and was paralyzed from the waist down. He was unable to attend St. Mary's Grade School for most of his third and fourth grades. Later, after back surgery, he attended Owatonna High School over an intercom during ninth grade. Because his teachers convinced the school board that some of the big boys would be able to carry him outside in case of an emergency such as a fire drill, he was able to return to high school to complete his years with his classmates.

He went on to marry, have children, become the president
:elchair Pilot's Association, and one
' Maricopa County Fair in Phoenix,
ts first general manager. Tom and
been long-lasting.
arol to John, who took her to the prom
:ually John became a priest; each year
nas greetings.
this would influence her in later life,
. She was asked to pray out loud before

ı member of Future Homemaker's of
, I was asked to prepare and deliver
ıefore the state banquet. It was a big
ırospect gave me stage fright. I told
ıf my trepidation. Dad invited our new
ılvester Brown, to come to our home to
gh still lacking confidence, I felt proud
ıosen. I delivered the prayer.

171

When Carol attended a week-long Future Homemaker's of America camp on a lake in the wilderness, the directors asked Carol to stay an additional week to help during the next week's FHA adventure. Her parents thought it was a good idea.

> **CAROL:** *Between the time one group of campers left and another group of girls arrived, I disappeared. No, I wasn't out with the only boy in camp nor was I lost in the woods. I had been introduced to canoeing, my newest love. A sunny day on a placid lake mesmerized me. Slipping into a life jacket, I rowed across the lake. I took a long time before returning. Standing on the shore were the camp directors, a husband-wife team, watching me approach. I knew, by the look on their faces, that the directors were shaken and worried by my absence.*

Carol pondered what to do after graduating from high school. What to be? What to do? She thought about several different things.

> **CAROL:** *As a senior in high school, I explored my options. Because stewardesses seemed to have an exciting life, I expressed my interest in pursuing that career. We called for an appointment with an airline representative. Sitting around the living room table, the representative explained to Mom, Dad, and me the work, the education I would need, and the adventures I might experience when flying. I was excited. However, Dad's reaction to the information was quite different. He did not think this lifestyle would suit me. I was very disappointed but didn't question him. I simply obeyed.*

Carol pictured herself happily married to Ron—the fellow she was dating during her senior year. But one evening as she and her dad finished chores, he turned to her and said, "I think you should stop seeing Ron."

172

CAROL: Again, I did not ask why, but simply obeyed, although my heart was broken. I was very upset by this abrupt ending to a budding romance with a great guy. *Was it because he was not Catholic?* That would have been a sign of the times and people's attitude toward intermarriage.

Following Rose's footsteps, Carol attended the University of Minnesota but only for two quarters. In early February, she received a letter from Dad saying he would be unable to pay tuition and needed her help on the farm. He also mentioned that he'd be driving Cathy and a few of her friends to Mankato where many communities of Sisters would have kiosks so young women could learn about convent life. And maybe Carol would decide to become a nun. Carol remembers laughing heartily with her roommate at that suggestion. It was her younger sister, Cathy, who talked about joining the convent. It had never occurred to Carol.

However, she did ride along to the gathering. Twenty or thirty different religious communities had representatives present to talk about its community's culture. She spent a great deal of time visiting with Sister Patrick Joseph from St. Benedict's Monastery in St. Joseph, Minnesota.

CAROL: *One night I entered Dad's bedroom, crying, "Dad, I want to join St. Benedict's Convent."*

I thought he would say no, but he surprised me, "I've always prayed that one of my daughters would become a nun."

Weeks passed during that summer. Field work was completed. Sister Patrick Joseph wrote weekly letters and included brochures about convent life. Carol carefully studied these and read books on convent life from the Sacred Heart Church library.

173

CAROL: *At the end of Rose's final year at the University, our family attended an engagement party at the Newman Center for Rose and Dick. I met Wally, Dick's brother. Wally made arrangements to come to the farm to visit with me during the summer. As we sat on the front lawn, I told him I was thinking about joining the convent. His answer stunned me, "Every good Catholic boy and girl ponders this question," he said. It made me think.*

Engagement Party: Back: Dad, Irma Trochlil; Front: Mom holding Lori, Rose, Dick, Wally, Carol

Carol's thoughts about the religious life continued to surface during that summer. Meanwhile, plans for Rose's wedding in September 1959 were in full swing. That same weekend, an unexpected turn in Carol's plans involved some quick thinking and action. Right before Rose's wedding, Carol discerned the direction for her life.

CAROL: *Four days before Rose's wedding, I approached Dad to talk about my future plans: I told him I'd decided that I really did want to join St. Ben's. His mind began churning. Dad said, "College started there this week. We should call Father Brown to help us make plans with the Sisters to see whether you can begin classes two weeks late."*

174

The very next night (Saturday before the big wedding, mind you), Father Brown was sitting at our kitchen table. I agreed Father Brown should make arrangements with the Sisters for my late arrival.

Rose was married on a Tuesday. Tuesday was convenient for both the couple and the wedding guests. Weddings were not usually held on weekends. Saturday was a busy day for farmers to go into town to do business and shopping. They could arrange to be away from field work more readily during the week. This was most convenient for the engaged couple. They continued their summer jobs until Friday, were married Tuesday, had a four-day wedding trip and moved on Sunday to Michigan.

The Sunday after the wedding Mom and Dad drove Carol to St. Ben's to begin her new life.

CAROL: *Dad, Mom and I made the four-hour trip to St. Ben's, which was essentially my home for the next nineteen years.*

So, Mom and Dad's two oldest daughters both began their new lives—away from their beloved farm home.

During her first year in the convent, Carol came home for two weeks for Christmas vacation. The furnace room—once the bulky furnace was replaced—was big enough that we sometimes used a part of it for other things. Carol had a sewing session with a couple of her former high school and university friends who joined her for an overnight. The room provided privacy for girl talk, which they shared with gusto. But it was a sad time too, for it was the last time she saw some of these dear friends.

175

LIVES CHANGE

Mom enjoyed vacationing with our family and with other relatives and friends. Although she was enthusiastic and eager for adventure, she tended to be unaware of danger. Once as she reached to touch the nose of a Kentucky Derby horse, Dad rescued her from a possible nasty wound when he grabbed her away and showed her the sign saying, "This horse bites."

Mom seemed to have no fear. She wasn't afraid of bats, garter snakes, or spiders. Once when Aunt Ag and Uncle Joe were vacationing with Mom and Dad, Mom approached an alligator near water's edge. The apparently sleeping animal opened its wide jaws. Hearing much yelling and screaming, Mom leaped back just in time to escape injury. Later, Aunt Ag teased her with an alligator postcard saying, "Don't pet the alligators."

> **ROSE:** *Like Mom, I am unafraid to try new things. After taking flying lessons, I made my solo flight. Awesome. Both parents encouraged travel, explorations, and experiencing new things in new places.*

Our parents visited most of the states in the contiguous United States. Throughout their years, they invited Carol to

176

travel to Hawaii with them. They visited Cathy in Alaska. They traveled with AA friends to international conferences and with other relatives and friends to fish and to play cards. Mom enjoyed Utah's views from the heights when she went mountain climbing with Carol. She enjoyed all rides, including the roller coaster at Steele County Free Fair and Disney World in Florida. Meanwhile, Dad enjoyed watching her have fun but did not join in these escapades.

After their retirement, one of us girls and/or a grandchild or friend was invited along to help Dad drive to or from their retirement home in Florida. Tourist sites were always part of our travel time. Carol recalls some of the stops returning from Florida.

After stopping for Mass at Kissimee, we played games of Yahtzee and Shit on your Neighbor. The rides at Walt Disney World were new, exciting, and enjoyable. We visited the Busch Gardens where we saw the giraffes, parrots, flamingos, and the elephant and orangutan shows. We stopped at Mission Nombre De Dios in St. Augustine and tangled with the Atlantic waves at Daytona Beach.

Dad made a special stop to view the aircraft carrier Yorktown, located at Charleston Harbor in Mt. Pleasant, South Carolina. We relished the Magnolia Gardens. Grandson Tom, his buddy Ken, and Carol accompanied Mom and Dad on this trip. Ken picked the forbidden camellia. Maybe it had fallen from the tree, but we spied it in his back pocket. The cypress knees and Chinese wisteria impressed us in the Cypress Gardens. The azaleas and camellias were in full bloom. We toured the Grand Ole Opry in Nashville, Tennessee, and spent Easter Sunday praising God at St. Meinrad's Archabbey in Indiana.

CAROL: *In mid-March of 1977, Tom, Rose's oldest son, and I accompanied Dad and Mom on their trip back to Minnesota. Dad went to the men's room at one of our stops. Twenty miles after our departure from the gas station, we realized he was not in his recliner in the* *back of the pick-up. Tom and I will never forget that experience. We turned around on that two-lane road and retraced our miles. We knew where we'd find him, but it didn't keep us from worrying. Upon our return, Dad was sitting calmly on a chair outside the station. He had told the owner that he knew we'd return for him because "I have the money."*

In the late 1940s and early 1950s, the atmosphere in our home changed from its earlier happy years. Our parents struggled to make farm payments, machinery payments, payments for food and clothing for the family. More and more money was spent for beer and alcohol.

Dad and Mom had more and more disagreements about money wasted on alcohol and no longer available for food or clothing. Farming is a hard, lonely business. The difficulties loom far greater when coupled with the disease of alcoholism.

CAROL: *When I was ten or eleven years old, Mom, Dad and I went shopping in town. While Mom and I waited in the car, Dad stopped at Hoff's Bar for a drink. We waited. And we waited. And we waited. Finally, Mom said, "Carol, go on in and tell your father it's time to go home." Hoff's Bar was dark inside, especially entering after being in the bright sunlight. I saw Dad standing with one foot up on the footrest, having a beer and visiting with other guys at the bar. Pulling on his sleeve, I looked up and said, "Mom says it's time to go home." He kept right on talking with his buddies. The bartender noticed my plight and offered me a piece of candy. Finally, Dad was ready and I walked out of the bar with Dad in tow. I was so relieved, but I also felt successful.*

Dad's whiskey bottle rode in the tool box on the tractor. He became more and more dependent on alcohol and less interested in food. During these days, we saw him trying

178

to vomit—dry heaves, because there was little food in his stomach.

Dad was sick. People were concerned about his health and his family. Several men told Dad about Alcoholics Anonymous (AA), a fairly new concept in our area. AA started in 1935 in Akron, Ohio. These men were AA members. They wanted to help Dad gain sobriety, too. Dad's barber accompanied Dad to his first AA meeting. Dad did not go to a treatment center, but for many days after his first meeting, men from AA spent long hours in our home as Dad adjusted to orange juice, coffee, and good food. Dad's sobriety was good for him and for our family.

Fortunately, in April 1954, just before Rose's senior year in high school and Carol's fourteenth birthday, Dad quit drinking, joined AA and tried to make up for the many times he'd not given us his best.

CAROL: *After he quit drinking, he took us out to eat—a rare treat. We drove a half mile north to the Monterey Ballroom, a combination ballroom and fine-dining establishment. The French chef, who knew her business, welcomed us to an otherwise empty room of dining tables outfitted with the finest linens, crystal, and silverware. Dad said we could order anything from the menu. We had not done this kind of thing before. What was I to order from such a list of good foods? I asked for lobster, unaware it was the priciest item on the menu. The chef invited us to come to the kitchen to watch her prepare the lobster and the dipping butter. I ate my dipped-in-butter lobster with relish, and Dad's eyes lit up as he watched me enjoy my first fine restaurant experience. This delicacy remains one of my favorite entrees.*

Dad gained serenity. It was obvious. We knew he was at peace within himself and with our Lord. Early in his years of sobriety, Carol found him reading at night.

179

CAROL: *One day when I was home from the convent, I noticed Dad reading something I'd never seen before. I commented, "How long have you been reading the Bible?"*

He said, "Since I made a retreat for alcoholics at St. John's Abbey. Sit down on the bed—here beside me, Carol. I want to tell you something. I haven't said this to many people because of what they might think. One evening when I was reading the Bible, I felt a presence in the room. Seated beside me was my visitor, Jesus."

I simply listened. I could tell this visitor touched Dad. I realized he had a relationship with Jesus that not only inspired me but also gave me goose bumps. I wanted to experience a friendship similar to his with this God who saved him from his need for drinking alcohol.

Earlier in her life Carol had tried to read the Bible but became frustrated after a few chapters.

CAROL: *When I was thirteen and sleeping in Rose's room, a Bible rested on the little table by her radio. I decided to read the whole thing. I did not know the Bible was comprised of many books. I began at the beginning. Genesis, Exodus and Numbers were ok, but when I reached Leviticus, I gave up. I wish someone had told me to start with Matthew, Mark, Luke, John, and Acts.*

In later years, my training in the convent gave me direction for daily meditation on a couple of Scripture paragraphs taken from the readings of the Mass. This prayer form, known as Lectio Divina, begins with listening—gently remembering (Lectio - Reading); then ruminating and reflecting (Meditatio - Meditation); followed by prayer (Oratio - Prayer); and finally, accepting Christ's embrace in the silent presence of

God (Comtemplatio - Contemplation). This prayer form became a lifelong habit and strengthened tangibly my ties to Dad.

Dad refused to miss any AA meetings, often taking in meetings in other nearby towns and in the Twin Cities. His good humor, likeable personality and encouraging ways engendered trust in many Owatonna alcoholics, who followed his steps into sobriety and the AA way of life.

A year or so after Dad became sober, Mom had a miscarriage. Dad gathered us girls around the kitchen table. With eyes opened wide, we viewed the small child as Mom unwrapped the freezer paper that held the tiny form of the child. Too surprised for words, we didn't even think about whether it was a boy or a girl.

In 1957, Mom was again pregnant. Dad knew her due date was imminent, but spring planting called him to prepare the fields for planting.

CAROL: *On an early May afternoon, when I was nearly seventeen years old, Mom moaned from the bedroom, "Tell Dad it's time. The baby's coming."*

Off I went to the fields to get Dad. However, he continued cultivating. He said, "I'll make one more round."

Mom groaned when I told her that he would come after he made one more round. True to his word, he came home, took a quick shower and took Mom to the hospital. Within a short time, he returned with news that we had a baby sister.

Dad figured that the chances of having another child (to carry his name) were very slim, as Mom was forty-five at the time of the baby's birth. He wanted a name close to his own. His name was Lawrence and many of his friends called him Larry. One of his old flames was named Lorinda. That

181

became the baby's baptismal name, which we shortened to Lori. Dad chose the middle name, Faith, to honor and thank God for his gift of sobriety.

Mom and Dad, even though they were in their forties, appeared and acted much younger after Lori's birth. She was with them always, even in the garden.

Dad, Lori and Mom

Cathy was fourteen when Lori was born. Growing rapidly, as children do, Lori soon learned to walk. Then Cathy started teaching her tricks.

CAROL: *Cathy, stretched out on her back on the front room floor (or sometimes on the kitchen floor), held Lori's feet in her hands on arms extended straight into the air. There stood Lori, our two-year old sister, grinning from east to west. One time Lori toppled onto her head. Fearfully, Cathy jumped up, grabbed Lori, stood her on the table and laughed until Lori got the giggles and forgot her bumps and pain.*

Cathy holding Lori

Rose and Carol moved from Minnesota in 1959. Our parents sold the farm in 1969.

Back: Rose, Carol, Cathy; Front: Mom, Lori, Dad

Dad had accepted a directorship for a new business in Pine City, Minnesota, at an alcoholic treatment center. By this time, Cathy was no longer living at home. Mom, Dad, and Lori moved from Steele County and found a lovely home with dark woodwork in the town of Pine City, Minnesota. Living in town was a different life style from anything either Mom or Dad had experienced. Dad plunged into his new career with great energy, Lori attended yet another school,

183

and Mom was home alone with no friends or relatives nearby and very little yard or garden work to be done. She filled some of her hours refinishing dressers for bedrooms.

A couple years later, Dad accepted a position to open a drug and alcoholic treatment center in St. Joseph's Hospital in Minot, North Dakota. Subsequently, Lori graduated from high school in Minot, North Dakota, not in Minnesota. Again, this transition to another home in a different city was difficult for Mom. She was no longer on a farm with open spaces for gardening and lawn care.

During the mid-1950s with the assistance of AA friends, Dad's health improved. However, Mom's illness became more and more obvious. There were times over the years on the farm that Mom's behavior baffled Carol.

> **CAROL:** *At times, Mom's behavior puzzled me. Her silence frightened me. Sometimes it lasted more than a day or two. Had I done something bad? Was I responsible? But I did not ask.*

Young eyes are observant and ears hear what is said.

> **CAROL:** *Once in the kitchen, I saw Mom, sitting on Dad's lap, laughing while teasing him. I was perplexed by what he said to her, "Elsie, be careful. You know how you will feel tomorrow morning."*

Long before her bipolar disorder was diagnosed, Dad sensed something was wrong as he observed her changing cycle of moods. He thought maybe she was having her period or, later, maybe going through menopause.

> **CAROL:** *Sometimes, Mom stopped going to Mass for a couple of Sundays in a row. I asked her, "Why didn't you go to Church with us?"*
>
> *She replied, "I was mixed up and angry. I didn't feel worthy of receiving communion."*

Her depression—part of the bipolar disorder—became nearly suicidal.

> **CAROL:** *Our water came from a cistern outside the mudroom window. The cistern was a very deep dark hole with a removable iron cover. Anyone who fell in would drown. When I was about ten years old, Mom and I were sitting on the bench by that very window. I asked Mom why she seemed so sad. She finally said, "Carol, I've been thinking about dropping myself into the cistern." She continued, "But I can't leave you, because I love you, your sisters and Dad." I was scared, but too young to know what to do.*

Because Dad's drinking was a concern for all of us, the atmosphere in our home was not always pleasant.

> **CAROL:** *One day I wandered into the bedroom and found Mom crying. I tried to comfort her and to understand why she was crying. Finally, I assumed it had something to do with Dad, so I asked her, "Why don't you divorce him?"*
>
> *Bewildered, she looked at me, "Where would I go? I love him."*

Before the onset of and even during Mom's struggles with bipolar disorder, she bestowed her talents upon us and taught us many important lessons. Her bipolar problems began as an adult with occasional episodes of mania and depression. These grew worse over the years. None of the family members realized the root cause of Mom's behavior swings. Each was confused by Mom's mood changes. By the time Lori reached her teenage years, things had become serious. Eventually, our once loving, energetic, reasonable, calm mother could no longer be reasoned with. Instead, she grew angry and silent. By the time she reached her sixties, she spent most of her nights and days in bed. At that point

Dad realized it was definitely time to get her diagnosed and treated.

Mom was hospitalized with depression in 1973. In this era, several people, family and doctors, had to sign papers stating it was necessary to commit this person for shock treatments.

When law enforcement officers, by court order from the doctors, arrived to take her to the hospital, they explained that she needed hospitalization. She sighed with relief and said, "Somebody does care." Diagnosed with manic depression—today known as bipolar disorder—she received shock treatments. Shock treatments did balance her emotions but seemed to eliminate memories.

When we were growing up, Mom said that the house was a place for family members, not pets. However, after her shock treatments, she changed her mind because Shea, a puppy that pre-teenager Lori and Sister Carol brought home to Minot, became a house pet. When the folks moved from Minot to Bemidji, Shea moved with them. Shea even traveled to and from the folks' Florida winter home—always staying in the trailer. Shea was a companion to Dad. One Floridian commented with surprise, "That dog stays by your side without a leash."

In Bemidji, a wild mother cat had kittens in the garage. Mom's lap became a resting place for the contented mother cat. She returned each spring to repeat her birthing actions in the garage, mothered the kittens there, but spent her off-hours resting peacefully in Mom's lap as Mom rested in her La-Z-Boy chair.

For the remainder of her life, she was a very quiet person who still enjoyed playing cards and the board game "Aggravation" which Dad called "dirty marbles" because someone was always pouncing on an opponent's marble and sending it to its starting position.

Dad enjoyed board games and card games, also, but was busy as director of the alcoholic and drug treatment center in St. Joseph's Hospital in Minot, North Dakota. Because the unit was drug-free and alcohol-free, Dad challenged doctors not to send patients who were receiving medications because medications are drugs. This was not easily accepted by some of the doctors but, nonetheless, Dad would not back down from this stipulation. (He had learned well from his AA friends that drugs of any sort as well as alcohol are addictive.)

Dad's health deteriorated in his early 60s when cancer struck in 1974 and his larynx was removed. Little did he know that after his *laryngectomy*, he himself would become addicted to one of his prescribed drugs—percodan. Pain radiated from his jaw down through his arm and up through his head. He took the medication, percodan, prescribed by doctors and became addicted. Three years after his 1974 surgery, he was hospitalized in a treatment unit in St. Paul where with the good counselors and God's grace, he was granted release from the percodan addiction. Now he was alcohol-free and drug-free.

When Mom and Dad were still living in Minot and he was recuperating from cancer surgery, Dad and Mom agreed that it was time to begin to disperse some of their belongings. Dad was concerned that he would soon die and he wanted us to choose items in the house that belonged to him and Mom. This was because when his mother died in 1955, Dad had a disappointing experience. Grandma Deml and he talked about her TV being his someday. Because the TV was not earmarked as Dad's and because Dad was hospitalized at the time of Grandma's death, another sibling got the TV. Dad wanted to prevent that kind of experience for us.

In 1974, Carol, Cathy and Lori were visiting the folks in their Minot home; Rose was absent. Holding three straws broken at different lengths, Dad told us, "The one who gets the longest straw chooses an item from the house; the one drawing the medium-long straw chooses next; the one with the shortest straw chooses last." He invited us to make two rounds. He encouraged us to take our treasured items home as soon as possible.

CAROL: *Because I had only a bedroom in the convent, I chose Mom's cedar chest which came from Grandpa and Grandma Wesely and a rocking chair that belonged to Grandma Deml.*

ROSE: *I chose the silver-plated tableware that mom had stored in the buffet. Many times the silverware had enhanced her table setting and had complimented a beautiful etched set of water glasses that were carefully preserved over the years. To this day, I continue to use the silver.*

However, cancer did not cause Dad's death in 1974. Dad and Mom moved again. Location, location, location. The peaceful acreage in Bemidji, where Mom and Dad moved shortly following his retirement after his surgery, brought many happy hours to our parents. As years went by, Dad and Mom gardened and grew flowers around their home. People would often stop to look at their lovely yard. Again, Mom enjoyed sharing flowers, many more than the lilacs she shared with her neighbors on the farm.

Both Mom and Dad improved and beautified their property, our home. Constructing new and improving existing buildings became one of Dad's goals over the years. The projects on the farm and later on their lake property in Bemidji became his reason to keep on moving, living one day at a time.

Even after many surgeries on his back and during his twenty-year struggle with pain after his laryngectomy, he sought new ventures Always ready to try something new, he purchased land bordering two separate lakes north of Bemidji, Minnesota. He acquired a fishing resort on one lakeshore. Lori and her family moved onto the property to help run the resort.

Along with that purchase, he also secured over a thousand acres of land. With Cathy's able assistance, he went into the real estate business. He divided and sold lakeside lots. Carol asked Dad why he had bought this piece of land and whether it was because of the lakes. He told her, "I've always been a fisherman at heart. I've also wanted to buy and sell land and, at last, I had the opportunity."

He single-handedly built a cabin for one of his lakeshore properties. However, he hadn't taken into consideration moving the building from the shed after it was built. Some dismantling took place. Then the cabin was moved to its lake location and sold as part of the parcel of land to one of his real estate customers.

Behind their Bemidji home was an acre of land that belonged to them. To reach this acre of land, Dad had to circle around almost two miles from behind because the land behind the house was too steep to climb. He built steep steps going up to this acre of land. Wonder of wonders, a patch of raspberries—his favorite—grew up there. These steps started at the same ground level as the house and extended far above the house. He named the steps "Stairway to Heaven."

Although his body hurt, his active mind would not be still. Someone suggested that he write the story of his life. The project was going along, but Dad was frustrated. He told Carol his dilemma, "I start writing and think of another idea and worry I will forget it."

"Dad," Carol said, "Go down town and buy some three-by-five cards, write your new idea and then go on writing the story you began earlier." He went to town that afternoon and succeeded in writing his book, "*I Carried You.*"

Mom and Dad lived in Bemidji for twenty years, at which time they again moved. This time their new residence was St. Therese Assisted Living in New Hope, Minnesota. While there, Carol took Dad to her doctor. Her doctor discovered that Dad had TMJ and told Dad that TMJ could be fixed. Thus, all his pain of the past twenty years would disappear. However, Dad had learned to live with the radiating pain and was now in his mid-80s. He wanted no more surgeries. He died six months later in 1996.

CAROL: *Mom and I were going through her picture albums after Dad died. I thought she might want to destroy one photo of Dad, in bed on his last hospital stay, on their 60th wedding anniversary. Her unselfish response to my question was, "I want to keep the picture because I never want to wish him back. He suffered so much."*

Mother had shock treatments the year before Dad's laryngectomy and this treatment changed her into a peaceful woman, although we missed her active mind—a loss of memory caused by shock treatments. She died in 2005.

CAROL: *Reflecting back over the years she suffered with this illness, I began to understand that some of Mom's earlier behaviors were unrelated to any of us. I believe that portions of Psalms 42 and 43 exemplify Mom's unspoken plea for help during the pain of her illness and the ultimate finding of peace with God's grace:*

Why are you downcast, my soul; why do you groan within me?

Wait for God, for I shall again praise him, my savior and my God.

On the day of her funeral in 2005, Psalm 84 spoke to me of her trust in God's promises:

As the sparrow finds a home and the swallow a nest to settle her young,

My home is by your altars, Lord of hosts, my king and my God!

We can never fully understand our own actions and reactions, much less those of others. So much comes from accepting God's plan even though we may never understand

190

His plan or have it revealed to us in our own lifetime.

Both Mom and Dad lived rich, full lives and loved life and each other as they struggled with their problems. During our childhood, they set an example: Their faith and commitment were an inspiration to follow and to bequeath to our families and others.

> **ROSE:** *Mom rarely expressed her feelings, her physical pains or her desires. I always remember how people simply gravitated to her because she knew how to listen with an open heart.*

Carol's life changed as well.

> **CAROL:** *I left the convent in 1978. Looking back, I think my giving in, without question, to Dad's suggestions about my future was a sign of my lack of independence, direction, and self-confidence. I had an overwhelming need to meet his expectations and receive his approval. So, I became a nun perhaps more to please my father than because it was my dream.*
>
> *I taught at an elementary school and married three years later. Bill Sisterman and I adopted two Korean brothers aged three and a half and five. When our children were small, I asked Bill to stop at the farm in Owatonna where I grew up. After knocking several times and waiting patiently, no one came to the door. However, as we were leaving the circle drive, a truck pulled in. The woman rolled down her window, calling, "Can I help you?"*
>
> *"Yes. I want to show Bill and the boys where I grew up."*
>
> *"You can't be a daughter of Lawrence and Elsie Deml. Your name was never mentioned."*

"I was in the convent when the folks sold the farm, so my name probably never popped up."

Finally, she agreed to show us the house. I marveled at changes she made on the main level and asked if we could see the upstairs. She hesitated, but took us upstairs. Changes were evident here too. Walls were removed. Instead of three small bedrooms and a hallway, one big room faced us.

Before going too far into the room, I asked, "Do you still have the attic?

"Yes," she replied, "Why do you ask?"

"I wondered if you still have bats there."

Unbelieving and astounded, she searched my face and exclaimed, "You DID live here, didn't you?"

Carol noticed another change that astonished her.

CAROL: *As I toured our former farm home, I noticed that the new owners had made a change. The route from the master bedroom to the bathroom now sported a direct passage through the closet. For all the years we lived there, Mom and Dad circled through the living room, kitchen, and back room to reach the bathroom. What a shame that they did not envision this short cut.*

REMEMBERING

On the farm, we had a life that was sometimes quite hard but also was very rich in many ways.

Dad, a teacher-at-heart, wanted us girls to know about many things in life—both of joy and sadness. He watched for ways to teach us about life as we grew old enough to understand the ramifications that might influence our understanding and acceptance of heartbreak and tragedy.

Tragedies sometimes result from events of weather. Our farm was very near "Tornado Alley." This was an expression that described the frequency of tornadoes that caused much destruction in southern Minnesota. Mother Nature can cause great loss of farm buildings and loss of crops in farming communities.

> **ROSE:** *Dad frequently told the story of the wind blowing and forcing tiny wisps of straw deep into wooden panels. He drove me to Waseca one bright spring morning to view destruction of buildings in the town of Waseca about fifteen miles from our farm. I recall marveling at the weather. It seemed so ironic that beautiful bright sunny days would follow a severe storm.*

CAROL: *Another time, Dad knew a tornado had hit a farm a few miles from our home. He invited all of us to go to the site and see the damage. We viewed the farm buildings from the country road, about a half-mile from the destroyed home. Shattered! It taught us to pray for the occupants and to be grateful for how we were saved from this destruction.*

Great tragedies may also be caused by human error or faulty mechanics. We had no television, but the scenes we viewed could not have been more graphic than today's on-the-scene coverage. There was a plane crash in the winter several miles east of our farm.

ROSE: *I actually walked through the snow-covered corn stubble with Dad. There were body parts, such as a finger in a glove, a broken separated part of an arm, scattered torn clothing as well as broken pieces of the shattered and scattered airplane in the field. By this time, most things had been removed, and I do not recall any other people walking in the field. How different from an accident scene of today that would be surrounded with yellow tape and searched and researched piece-by-piece for various pieces of evidence. I even recall the roads we traveled to get there.*

CAROL: *Another plane crash! A two-seater plane went down in a nearby field. Dad showed us the accident from the road and we discussed the situation. Although it was a terrible sight with pieces of the plane for miles around, I have never been fearful of flying.*

Death was a part of life and Dad and Mom taught us to believe in an afterlife. When someone faced death, we learned to accept death as a part of God's loving plan—not something to fear.

CAROL: *We girls were taken to Grandma Deml's bedside, when she was dying of cancer. We visited with her for a while, then knelt by her bed and prayed with her for her happy death.*

Rural Minnesota has become a very different world. Not only have farm sizes and equipment changed, but even the farm buildings and sites have altered dramatically. When Rose returned to the farm in the spring of 2012 to take pictures, she introduced the farm to Joshua, Lori's eldest son. She wanted Josh to see the farm where Lori, his mom, lived the early years of her life.

Our family lived through an era of great change in farming and farm life—from horse-drawn plows to huge combines. Small family farms began disappearing as they were amalgamated into bigger and bigger farms.

But it was a great life, if a hard one, that we lived. We all worked very hard on the farm—not just our mother and father, but all of us girls. We girls worked harder than many other farm girls because there were no sons to help Dad.

ROSE: *The oldest of four girls in my family, I worked as Dad's "right-hand" or "hired man," helping with daily chores and working in the fields. The other girls helped as they grew older. We four girls were spread out in age. Lori, my baby sister, was born when I was twenty, Carol was nearly seventeen and Cathy almost fourteen. Now we were four girls in the family. Two and a half years later, Lori was the flower girl in my wedding.*

Carol, Cathy, Lori and Rose

I always smiled when Mom was asked about her family. She would always say that she had three daughters and the baby.

Because Mom and Dad encouraged us, all four girls did graduate from college. Sending children—especially daughters—to attend college was a major accomplishment and source of pride for any family back then.

One rare occasion, some twenty years later, we four sisters were together and having an all-night gab session. Lori suddenly spoke up and said that she lived in a different era and did not have any of our memories of the farm.

Rose had questions about the recurring unfinished dreams of life on the farm. She tried to recall places and incidents to answer these questions. Dreams, her old Kodak photos, and conversations nudged Rose's memory. Asking questions, Carol used her Kodak photos and visiting with Rose to recall vivid scenes from childhood. We now put together our memories to share.

Some of the farm buildings are gone today, but the land remains. We learned many lessons from our parents. And even their illnesses—or the way they dealt with them—

196

provided us with valuable insights. Some of our folks' harsh diseases and ailments were "visible" to the outside world: alcoholism, back pain, and cancer. Then there was mother's bipolar disorder, mostly unknown to other people—although it caused a lot of heartache, especially for Dad and Lori, who suffered through the most trying times.

> **CAROL:** *In writing these pages, I've become more aware of Dad's building prowess. I am amazed at the building projects he completed. His mind, physical strength and temperament seemed unaffected by his alcohol consumption.*

Even though Dad was constantly challenged physically, his body remained strong over the years. Larry, one of Rose's sons, recalled his amazement at his grandpa's strength. "I was around eighteen years old, the prime of my life, as they claim. And I was fishing with grandpa years after his cancer surgery. We were out on the dock. The boat wouldn't start; the battery was dead. So Grandpa, nearly seventy years old, got a vice grip pliers and knelt on the dock. He reached down into the boat with the vice grip pliers, clamped onto one post of the battery and yanked the battery out of the boat with one arm. I don't think I could have lifted that battery with two arms. And he did that after all of his operations. I will always remember him as a very big man. I am taller than he (he claimed to be shrinking). I weighed more than he, but he said he weighed 240 in his prime. I weigh 220 now. I will always remember how strong he was at that time."

Throughout our parents' lives, we were blessed with their dedication to beauty, honesty, and Christian grace. They were gracious and accepting of all the people they knew. Mom had a gentle way of making things beautiful.

A Tribute to Mom

Twinkling twice and then quiet

Lightning-fast over piano keys

Washing, rinsing, wiping dishes

Rubbing, scrubbing ceiling, tub, floors

Embroidering pretty pictures onto towels

Crocheting colorful edges onto handkerchiefs

Ripping, piecing and braiding rag rugs

Darning holes in socks

Touching hands once were smooth but

Now are scarred and worn with age

Rubbing, scratching, massaging Dad's tired back

Wiping away tears of children and grandchildren

Tears tumbling down cheeks

Hugging, cuddling, soothing too-deep wounds

Yours are talented hands, Mother

Author: Carol Sisterman

Besides that, she thought of others' needs.

CAROL: *Mother's beautiful flower gardens pleased her. New plants intrigued her. She graciously shared her plants and flowers.*

She treasured books and shared that pleasure by reading aloud to us as children. She also read to Dad during his many painful recoveries from surgery.

We caught their spirit of service. In particular, serving alcoholics and their loved ones became an everyday occurrence for Mom and Dad after Dad gained sobriety. Two Alcoholics Anonymous sayings, "Let go and let God" and Thy will be done," were favorites of Dad's. And, over the years, we found in them much wisdom and guidance for our own lives.

> **ROSE:** *True to their marriage commitment, "'Til death do us part," Mom and Dad celebrated sixty years of marriage. Dad lived a few weeks beyond that day.*
>
> *Always the love of his life, Mom died on Valentine's Day nine years later. The folks were an inspiration of love and commitment to all who knew them.*

The greatest legacy Mom and Dad gave us was living out their faith. Their example is taught in the words of St. Paul in Philippians 4:8:

Whatever is true, whatever is honorable,

whatever is just, whatever is pure,

whatever is lovely, whatever is gracious,

if there is any excellence and

if there is anything worthy of praise,

think about these things.

Rose Deml Trochlil, Carol Deml Sisterman